USAF HISTORICAL STUDIES

THE GERMAN AIR FORCE IN WORLD WAR II

LIST OF PUBLICATIONS AVAILABLE IN THE SERIES

USAF HISTORICAL STUDIES: NO. 189

Historical Turning Points in the German Air Force War Effort

By Richard Suchenwirth

With an Introduction by Telford Taylor

USAF HISTORICAL DIVISION
RESEARCH STUDIES INSTITUTE
AIR UNIVERSITY

ARNO PRESS · NEW YORK

Reprinted with the cooperation of the Department
of Defense and the Historical Division, the Air
University of the United States Air Force.

Library of Congress Catalog Card No.: 68-22554

Manufactured in the U.S.A.
by Arno Press, Inc., New York, 1968

INTRODUCTION TO THE SERIES

The publication of this series of official historical studies is at once a most significant contribution to our knowledge of the Second World War and a landmark in the development of commercial publishing.

So much is published nowadays—far beyond the capacity of any individual even to screen—and so much is printed that ought never to see the light of day, that one tends to forget the considerable amount of writing well worth reading which rarely or never gets published at all. These volumes are an excellent example. Military monographs by foreign officers whose names are unknown to the public are not attractive items to most commercial publishing houses. But sometimes, as in the present case, they are unique sources of information which should be available in public if not in private libraries. Less often, and again as in the case of these volumes, they are surprisingly well written, and in many parts fascinating to the general reader as well as to the historian or military specialist.

The foreword of the Air Force Historical Division describes the inception and purposes of its German Air Force Historical Project and the circumstances under which these studies were written. Together with others to be published or made available for research in the future, the fruits of the Project are an analytic survey, at once comprehensive and intensive, of the Luftwaffe's structure and operations.

Not the least remarkable feature of the series is its authorship. With the single exception of Dr. Richard Suchenwirth—a one-time Austrian Army Officer and more recently a historian and educator in Munich—they are all former Luftwaffe generals, of low to middling seniority, who were intimately and responsibly involved with the events and problems of which they write. All seven were born within the decade 1891–1901, and thus in their forties or early fifties during most of the war years. Lieutenant-colonels or colonels when the war began, they filled a wide variety of staff and administrative assignments. Only two (Deichmann and Drum) attained three-star rank (*General der Flieger*), and only one (Deichmann) was ever given a major field command.

In military parlance, accordingly, they are all "staff" rather than "command" types, and for present purposes that is a good thing. Staff officers are responsible for the smooth functioning of the military machine; they must anticipate and provide for contingencies, and are expected to possess good powers of analysis and imagination. They spend much time drafting orders, which requires the ability to write with clarity and brevity. All these qualities are reflected in their product; our seven generals must have been good staff officers.

Banned by the Treaty of Versailles, the German air arm was condemned to a clandestine and embryonic life until 1933, and the Luftwaffe's existence was not publicly acknowledged until 1935. Hermann Goering and his colleagues in its command thus had only six years prior to the war in which to assemble and organize an officer corps. Its younger members—those who were lieutenants and captains when the war came—were recruited and trained during those years (1933–39), but the upper reaches of the corps had to be manned in other ways.

The need for experienced staff officers was especially acute, and this was met largely by transferring army (and a few navy) officers to the newly established air arm. Thus it is not surprising to find that all but one (Morzik) of our generals were professional soldiers who made their careers in the *Reichsheer* of the Weimar Republic, and received general staff training at the time Adolf Hitler was coming to power. So far as possible, the officers to be transferred were selected from those who had served in the air arm during the First World War, as had Deichmann and Drum.

Morzik alone represents the other principal type of senior Luftwaffe officer. He was not of the "officer class"; he had been a non-commissioned officer in the air arm during the First World War. Between the wars he led an adventurous and varied life as a commercial pilot, a successful competitor in aviation contests, a Junkers test pilot, and a flying instructor. Like his more famous superiors—Udet, Loerzer, von Greim, and Goering himself—Morzik was a free-lance knight of the air, and one of a considerable company commissioned from civil life in the 1933–35 period.

These generals are writing about events of which they were a part, in the course of a war in which Germany was catastrophically, and the Luftwaffe even ignominiously, defeated. What they have written is certainly not objective in the sense that it is detached; they see with the eyes and speak the language of the air arm, and readily find explanations for their own failures in the mistakes of the Army leadership—often with good reason, to be sure. But their work is objective in the sense that it is dispassionate. Their studies bespeak a deep curiosity about their conduct of the war and the causes of their defeat, and they have, on the whole, endeavored to put the record straight by the lines they are able to perceive.

There is, however, a great deal that they did not perceive. Few, if any, are those who can write at length about other men without revealing a great deal about themselves, and our authors are not in this respect exceptional. At least during this century, the German military profession has been rightly celebrated for its technical and tactical competence, but its record in the field of grand strategy has been abysmal. By and large these studies do not often venture into the rarefied atmosphere of the highest levels of command, and when they do, the results are unimpressive. Plocher's account of the reasons for the German attack against the Soviet Union,[1] for example, is superficial and diffuse. Of course he was not party or privy to the decision, but in telling us what he has heard there is little effort to winnow fact from fable, or to assess the considerations and alternatives.

In other respects, these volumes are not to be faulted so much for what is said as for what is left unspoken. Describing the Russian soldier, Uebe tells us that it is his "inherent character" to be "ruthless" and to place "a relatively lower value on human life" than "Western" peoples do.[2] For myself, I am inclined to discount popular stereotypes about national characteristics, and to judge rather upon a record of behavior. Beyond question the Russian soldier was often ruthless and worse, but what of the German soldier in Russia? Neither Uebe nor any of his colleagues carries the story in that direction. To be sure the Luftwaffe, by the nature of its operations, was not much involved in the exterminations, forced labor impressments, and other atrocities in which the Army was extensively implicated. But this hardly justifies Plocher's chest-thumping conclusion that: ". . . the incom-

[1] Plocher, *The German Air Force versus Russia, 1941*, pp. 1–3 (1965).
[2] Uebe, *Russian Reactions to German Airpower in World War II*, p. 1 (1964).

parable performances of the individual German soldier in combat in the East are above criticism. This applies to all ranks, from the lowest private to general officers, on the land, in the air, and on the seas."[3] Unhappily, the German military records tell quite a different story.

Fortunately such departures from the factual dimension are rare, and the authors have given us a unique and invaluable fund of information. Two of these studies concern the high command of the Luftwaffe, and two more cover particular Luftwaffe functions —air lift and ground support. The remaining six all concern the fighting on the eastern front between the German and Russian forces—a ferocious conflict on a scale greater than any other in human history.

Three of the eastern front studies, all by Plocher, constitute a chronological account of Luftwaffe operations on the eastern front in 1941, 1942, and 1943, one year to each volume. It is a mammoth undertaking of nearly 1,200 pages, well organized, and abundantly supported and illustrated with maps, charts, and photographs.

Plocher was chief of staff of an air corps on the southern part of the front, and remained in the east until the middle of 1943. Thus he witnessed at first hand the Luftwaffe's highly successful operations during the first few days of the campaign in July 1941, in the course of which the entire Russian air force was virtually annihilated, as well as the great encirclements at Minsk, Kiev, Bryansk, and elsewhere, which netted over two and a quarter million Russian prisoners and drove the Soviet forces back to the gates of Leningrad and Moscow and the banks of the Don. No doubt the Wehrmacht's failure to achieve decisive success was more the fault of the Army leadership than of the Luftwaffe, but the air generals made serious mistakes of their own, of which Plocher stresses two of major strategic proportions: (1) failure to carry out strategic bombing attacks on Russian armaments industries, and (2) dispersion of the slender air strength at the extreme northern end of the front, so that Murmansk and Archangel remained in Russian hands, as ports through which the western Allies could help the Russians to recover, following their nearly disastrous losses in the opening months of the campaign.

With the Russian air arm largely destroyed and strategic operations neglected, the Luftwaffe became, in practical terms, part of the German army—"flying artillery," supplemental transportation, additional ground forces. There were few Russian aircraft for the German *Flak* to shoot at, so the anti-aircraft units became front-line artillery.

Later on, as the Army got into even deeper trouble, the Luftwaffe was pulled in after it. Bombers were misused on ground-attack and airlift assignments; efforts to supply encircled German armies by air caused the Luftwaffe catastrophic losses. New Russian aircraft began to appear on the scene, and the balance gradually shifted so that by the end of 1943 the Germans no longer enjoyed air superiority, and the Luftwaffe became, as Plocher puts it, a "fire brigade," constantly on emergency call to plug up holes or salvage hard-pressed Army units.

How the Russians responded to the Luftwaffe's operations is the subject of Uebe's report. Except for the first few days, when the Soviet planes were destroyed in close array on their own airfields, like our own aircraft on Clark Field in the Philippines in December 1941, the Russians reacted to the overwhelming German superiority with great adaptability, and skill in the arts of camouflage and deception. Rails laid on ice did not sink with the thaw, for supports had been built under the ice; ships that appeared half-sunk and useless were under repair, with the bow flooded to elevate the stern. "As events show," writes

[3] Plocher, *The German Air Force versus Russia, 1943,* p. 266 (1967).

Uebe, "Russian reaction to German Air Force operations, however primitive and make-shift in character, and however crude they might have first appeared to be to their more enlightened Western opponents, proved throughout the course of the war to be highly efficient, effective, and ultimately an important factor in the defeat of Germany." A lesson for the American military command in Vietnam?

These same qualities were strikingly manifest in the Russian partisan operations behind the German lines, as described in a short but vivid study by General Karl Drum. The partisan units depended on air transportation for reinforcements, leadership, supplies, evacuation of wounded, and other necessary assistance, and all this was accomplished with obsolete aircraft and improvised equipment, utilizing air-drop or well-concealed air strips. Upon occasion, men were "delivered" to the partisans by parachuteless air-drop, wrapped in straw and dropped from low-flying planes into deep snow. The Germans, counting on a blitzkrieg victory, had made no preparations for anti-partisan warfare. No aircraft were earmarked to deal with the Russian air-supply, no single anti-partisan command was established to deal with the problem as a whole. Brutal occupation policies boomeranged by driving the population into the arms of the partisans. The German failure to take effective countermeasures is a striking demonstration that overwhelming superiority in heavy weapons and a sophisticated military tradition are no guarantee of success against surprise and deception.

Perhaps the most interesting and valuable of the eastern front volumes is Schwabedissen's extensive and perceptive study of the Russian air force as it appeared to the Germans. Through interchange of equipment and manufacturing and training facilities during the Weimar period, the antagonists were well known to each other. The Russian air performance in Spain and Finland had not been impressive, and in 1941, just prior to their attack, the Luftwaffe had a pretty accurate picture of the opposing force: it was far larger than the Luftwaffe, but much inferior in equipment, leadership, and training. The Germans expected to smash it to bits, and they succeeded.

What the Germans failed to reckon with was the Russians' recuperative powers. Most of their aircraft were destroyed on the ground rather than in the air, so that personnel losses were not high. The armament industries were rapidly moved eastward, and an early winter hampered Luftwaffe operations and gave the Russians a badly needed respite. By the winter of 1941–42 new Russian air units, better equipped, were beginning to appear at the front.

Still vastly superior in operational capacity, the Luftwaffe remained dominant in 1942, but in 1943 Russian numerical superiority, and techniques improved by experience, began to tell. During the last two years of the war, general air superiority passed to the Russian side of the front. But superior German technique enabled them to operate and achieve local successes right up to the end of the war; the Russians never achieved the total superiority enjoyed by the Allies on the western front.

German military air transport operations were opened by spectacular successes in the West. By parachute, glider, and landed aircraft, German airborne units descended on the major airfields of Norway and Denmark, on the airfields and tactically crucial bridges in Holland, and on the famous fort Eben Emael in Belgium. Morzik's fine account covers these operations in detail, as well as the later successful but costly assault on Crete, and the planned but never executed airborne operations in England, Gibraltar, Malta, and elsewhere.

The transport workhorse of the Luftwaffe was the three-engined Junkers 52, opposite number to our C-47s (otherwise known as DC-3s, Dakotas, "gooney birds," and now in Vietnam as "dragonships"), and well-known to all European travelers of ancient enough vintage to have flown Lufthansa during the thirties. A sturdy and versatile airplane, it was turned out by the thousands, but by the end of the war there were less than two hundred left. Most of the rest lay shattered and scrapped in Russia, near Demyansk and Stalingrad.

Morzik's account of the Demyansk and Stalingrad airlifts is gripping and enlightening. Retreating from the Moscow sector, the German Second Corps (roughly 100,000 men) was encircled at Demyansk in February 1942. Hitler forbade a breakout to the rear, and decided to supply the Corps by air. This was accomplished, but at a cost of 160 railway trains of gasoline, 265 Ju-52s, and consequent loss of trained crews and disruption of the pilot-training program. The psychological cost was even higher, for the apparent success of the operation made spuriously credible Goering's promise, ten months later, to supply Paulus' Sixth Army of over 300,000 men, encircled at Stalingrad. By then the Luftwaffe had only 750 Ju-52s left; half of them, and many bombers pressed into service as transports, were lost in the futile effort.

Airlift operations were the product of special circumstances, and strategic bombing the Luftwaffe neglected from birth to death. Day in and day out, its basic role was direct support of Army operations: attacking enemy troop columns, strong points, and tanks; impeding the flow of enemy reinforcements or cutting off their avenues of retreat; general intelligence reconnaissance. After 1941, Army support comprised over 75% of the Luftwaffe's operational activity—too large a proportion, as General Deichmann points out in his treatise "German Air Force Operations in Support of the Army." Deichmann traces the development of German air theory from its beginnings in the First World War, and explores the manner in which those theories shaped the Luftwaffe and governed its operational potential. The military air specialist will find this an exceptionally informative study.

In "The German Air Force General Staff," Nielsen takes us into the weird world of the Luftwaffe high command, well stocked with colorful characters, many of them adequately unattractive. Hitler was not much interested in air power and left Goering a free hand as long as things went well. After the period of spectacular initial successes, Goering suffered a sharp decline in influence, and the Fuehrer interjected himself into the Luftwaffe's management. He was not helpful; his decisions were the product of ignorance and favoritism and simply completed the process of demoralization.

Nielsen's study is focused on the general staff—i.e. the group of specially trained officers who held staff assignments—but its perspective is much broader, and includes the interplay of personality and rivalry at the top. Until his fall from grace, Goering's domination was complete, with one exception—Erhard Milch, his second-in-command, who had his own contacts and standing with Hitler and the Nazi Party. A former director of Lufthansa and a man of great energy and administrative ability, Milch was ambitious to the point that his attitude on proposed measures was governed less by the merits than by his estimate of their probable effect on his personal situation. Thus he initially opposed the creation of a general staff, and, when overruled, bent his energies to ensuring that the chief of the general staff would not impair his status as the No. 2 man. The consequence was a running battle between Milch and the succession of chiefs—seven during the Luftwaffe's less than twelve years of life—who served, basically, as Goering's advisors in the field of combat operations.

The results of his jerry-built command structure and riven leadership are graphically portrayed in Professor Suchenwirth's "Historical Turning Points in the German War Effort." Since the Luftwaffe ended the war in a state of total disintegration, the title postulates a study of crucial decisions which proved disastrous.

Perhaps the worst mistakes were made before the war began, and were the almost inevitable consequence of the personal shortcomings of the Luftwaffe leaders. Hans Jeschonnek—a career army officer barely old enough to have had a bit of flying experience at the very end of the First World War—was the Luftwaffe chief of staff from early 1939 to his suicide in 1943. Blindly devoted to Hitler and, until near the end, to Goering, he swallowed whole Hitler's assurances that the war would be a short blitzkrieg. Accordingly, he took no interest in training, neglected air transport, opposed the development of a long-range bomber, and focused all of his considerable ability on army support, and especially on the dive bomber. During the first year of the war these weaknesses did not show, but the Luftwaffe's failure over Britain and its inadequacy to the sustained demands of the eastern front were the direct result of such miscalculations, of which Jeschonnek was by no means the only author. Udet, Milch, Goering, and Hitler himself all contributed greatly to the Luftwaffe's misconstruction, misuse, and miserable fate.

In 1936, when Francisco Franco asked Hitler for help in moving his forces from Africa to Spain, Ju-52s were sent to do the job. Nine years later, as the Third Reich crumbled, Ju-52s—what was left of them—were still the standard Luftwaffe transport aircraft, and in this circumstance the Luftwaffe's intrinsic weakness is strikingly reflected. Messerschmitt 109s and 110s, Dornier 17s, Heinkel 111s, Ju-87 "Stukas," and Ju-88s were all on hand before the war began. With the sole exception of the Focke-Wulf 190—somewhat but not significantly superior to the Me 109—not a single new major aircraft type was added to the Luftwaffe until the last year of the war. Then came the first jet aircraft and the V-weapons, but it was too little and too late.

In retrospect, it is apparent that the Luftwaffe reached its peak of effectiveness before the war had even begun. Germany's bloodless conquest at Munich was achieved largely by the fear of Goering's bombers—a threat that was real enough, though exaggerated far beyond its true dimensions. Spectacular as they were, the Luftwaffe's triumphs in Poland, Norway, Holland, and even against the French (whose air force was woefully decrepit) were not scored against major opponents. As early as Dunkirk the veil was torn, and from then on the story is one of decline, gradual until the winter of 1941–42, rapid thereafter.

And so it came about that the story told, and well told, in these volumes can be fairly summarized in just seven words: how not to run an air force.

Telford Taylor

USAF HISTORICAL STUDIES: NO. 189

HISTORICAL TURNING POINTS IN THE GERMAN
AIR FORCE WAR EFFORT

by

Richard Suchenwirth

USAF HISTORICAL DIVISION
RESEARCH STUDIES INSTITUTE
AIR UNIVERSITY
JUNE 1959

FOREWORD

Historical Turning Points in the German Air Force War Effort by Professor Richard Suchenwirth, is one of a series of historical studies written by, or based on information supplied by, former key officers of the German Air Force for the United States Air Force Historical Division.

The overall purpose of the series is threefold: 1) To provide the United States Air Force with a comprehensive and, insofar as possible, authoritative history of a major air force which suffered defeat in World War II; 2) to provide a history of that air force as prepared by many of its principal and responsible leaders; 3) to provide a first-hand account of that air force's unique combat in a major war with the forces of the Soviet Union. This series of studies therefore covers in large part virtually all phases of the Luftwaffe's operations and organization, from its camouflaged origin in the Reichswehr, during the period of secret German rearmament following World War I, through its participation in the Spanish Civil War and its massive operations and final defeat in World War II.

The German Air Force Historical Project, (referred to hereinafter by its shorter and current title, "The GAF Monograph Project") has generated this and other especially prepared volumes which comprise, in one form or another, a total of nearly fifty separate studies, some of them in multi-volume form. The project, patterned, in part, after an Army program already in existence, was, upon recommendation of Headquarters Air University late in 1952, approved and funded by Headquarters USAF in early 1953. General supervision was assigned to the USAF Historical Division by Headquarters USAF, which continued principal funding of the project through 30 June 1958. Within the USAF Historical Division Dr. Albert F. Simpson and Mr. Joseph W. Angell, Jr., respectively, Chief and Assistant Chief of the Division, exercised overall supervision of the project. The first steps towards its initiation were taken in the fall of 1952 following a staff visit by Mr. Angell to the Historical Division, Headquarters United States Army, Europe at Karlsruhe, Germany. There, the Army, as has been mentioned, was conducting a somewhat similar historical project covering matters and operations largely of primary interest to that service. Whereas the Army's project had produced or was producing a multiplicity of studies of varying length and significance (more than 2,000 have been prepared by the Army project thus far), it was early decided that the Air Force should request a radically smaller number (less than fifty) which should be very carefully planned initially and rather closely integrated.

iii

Thirteen narrative histories of GAF combat operations, by theater areas, and 27 monographic studies dealing with areas of particular interest to the United States Air Force were recommended to and approved by Headquarters USAF in the initial project proposal of late 1952. (A list of the histories and studies appears at the end of this volume.)

By early 1953 the actual work of preparing the studies was begun. Colonel Wendell A. Hammer was assigned as Project Officer, with duty station at the USAREUR Historical Division in Karlsruhe. General der Flieger a. D. Paul Deichmann was appointed and served continuously as Control Officer for the German phase of the project; he also had duty station at the USAREUR Historical Division. Generalleutnant a. D. Hermann Plocher served as Assistant Control Officer until his recall to duty with the new German Air Force in the spring of 1957. These two widely experienced and high-ranking officers of the former Luftwaffe secured as principal authors, or "topic leaders," former officers of the Luftwaffe, each of whom, by virtue of his experience in World War II, was especially qualified to write on one of the thirty-nine topics approved for study. These "topic leaders" were, in turn, assisted by "home workers"--for the most part former general and field-grade officers with either specialized operational or technical experience. The contributions of these "home workers," then, form the basic material of most of the studies. In writing his narrative, the "topic leader" has put these contributions into their proper perspective. The Control Officer and the Project Editor (Mr. Edwin P. Kennedy, Jr.) have, when necessary, indicated the relationship of the particular subject matter of each study to the other studies included in the project.

These studies find their principal authority in their authors' personal knowledge and experience. Thus, these studies are neither unbiased nor are they "histories" in the ordinary sense of that word. Instead, they constitute a vital part of the story without which the final history of Germany's role in World War II cannot be written.

In preparing these studies, however, the authors have not depended on their memories alone. Instead, they have supplemented their knowledge with a collection of Luftwaffe documents which has come to be known as the Karlsruhe Document Collection and which is now housed in the Archives Branch of the USAF Historical Division. This collection consists of directives, situation reports, war diaries, personal diaries, strength reports, minutes of meetings, aerial photographs, and various other materials derived, chiefly, from three sources: the Captured German Documents Section of The Adjutant General in Alexandria, Virginia; the Air Ministry in London; and private German collections donated to the project by its participating authors and contributors.

In addition, the collection includes the contributions of the "home workers." Thus, the interested researcher can test the conclusions of the "topic leaders" against the basic documents or secure additional information on most of the subjects mentioned in the studies.

The authors have also made use of such materials as the records of the Nuremberg Trials, the manuscripts prepared by the Foreign Military Studies Branch of the USAREUR Historical Division, the official military histories of the United States and the United Kingdom, and the wealth of literature concerning World War II, both in German and English, which has appeared in book form or in military journals since 1945.

The complexity of the GAF Monograph Project and the variety of participation which it has required can easily be deduced from the acknowledgments which follow. On the German side: General der Flieger a. D. Paul Deichmann, who, as Chief Control Officer, became the moving force behind the entire project; Generalleutnant Josef Kammhuber, who heads the new German Air Force, and who has consistently supported the project; Generaloberst a. D. Franz Halder, Chief of the German Army General Staff from 1938 to 1942, whose sympathetic assistance to the Project Officer, the Project Editor, and the German Control Group is greatly appreciated; Generalfeldmarschall a. D. Albert Kesselring, who contributed to several of the studies and who also, because of his prestige and popularity in German military circles, was able to encourage many others to contribute to the project; and all of the German "topic leaders" and "home workers" who are too numerous to mention here, but whose names can be found in the prefaces and footnotes to the individual studies.

In Germany, Col. Wendell A. Hammer, USAF, served as Project Officer from early in 1953 until June, 1957. Colonel Hammer's considerable diplomatic and administrative skills helped greatly towards assuring the project's success. Col. William S. Nye, USA, was Chief of the USAREUR Historical Division at the project's inception. His strong support provided an enviable example of interservice cooperation and set the pattern which his several successors followed.

In England, Mr. L. A. Jackets, formerly Chief of Air Historical Branch No. 6 of the British Air Ministry and now Librarian, Air Ministry, gave invaluable assistance with captured Luftwaffe documents.

At the Air University, Maxwell Air Force Base, Alabama, a number of people, both military and civilian, have given strong and expert support to the project. Lt. Gen. Idwal H. Edwards, a former Commander of the Air University, initiated correspondence with Maj. Gen. Orlando Ward, USA, which resulted in a Department of the Army letter outlining the respective USAF-Army responsibilities for the project's execution. General Edward's interest in the project and its goals was matched by the assistance given by his successors: General Laurence S. Kuter, Lt. Gen. Dean C. Strother and Lt. Gen. Walter E. Todd.

Other personnel at Headquarters Air University who have given freely of their time and experience include: Dr. James C. Shelburne, Educational Advisor to the Commander; Mr. J. S. Vann, Chief of Special Projects Branch, DCS/Operations; and Mr. Arthur F. Irwin, Chief, Budget Division, DCS/Comptroller.

Col. Garth C. Cobb, both as Director of the Research Studies Institute of the Air University and, formerly, as Deputy Director of that organization, has helped to guide the project through a maze of administrative problems which, because of the project's unprecedented nature, have beset it from the beginning. Colonel Cobb's assistance, with that of his predecessors Col. Curtis D. Sluman, Brig. Gen. Clinton W. Davies and Col. Wilfred J. Paul, was invaluable to the project.

The project is grateful to Col. Fred W. Miller, USAF Air Attache to Germany, and the Assistant Air Attache, Lt. Col. Leonard C. Hoffmann, both of whom gave indispensable aid during the project's last year in Germany. Also in Germany, Mr. Joseph P. Tustin, the Historian of Headquarters, United States Air Forces in Europe, has ably assisted the project by solving a variety of logistical and administrative problems.

This study was translated by Mrs. Patricia Klamerth, whose skillful contribution to the project is greatly appreciated.

Mrs. Sally Watkins, responsible for the final typing, deserves special thanks for her extraordinary patience and competence.

Above all, the project is indebted to all of the members of the USAREUR Historical Division, the Office of the Chief of Military History, and the USAF Historical Division who, through direct assistance and advice, helped the project to achieve its goals.

Dr. Albert F. Simpson, Chief, USAF Historical Division, and Mr. Edwin P. Kennedy, Jr., the Project Editor, collaborated in the final editing of this study. To assure the technical accuracy of the translation, Mr. Kennedy compared the entire text with the original German manuscript. The stylistic peculiarities of the author, when they did not lend themselves to idiomatic English, were left in literal translation.

CONTENTS

vii

Structural theories and the strength and quality of materials are commonly tested in a laboratory by being subjected to abnormal stresses and strains. An engineer can learn a great deal from the resultant destruction of his testing material. Similarly, the student of air power can benefit by studying the destruction of the German Air Force in World War II, for the Luftwaffe's defeat meets at least some of the criteria of the laboratory test. In size and quality, the Luftwaffe was surpassed only by the United States Army Air Forces and the Royal Air Force. The test to which it was subjected, however, was in some ways more severe than that faced by any other major air force in World War II; and the collapse which resulted was complete.

War offers the only complete test of an air force. To the historian, the defeat of an air force--or any military machine--is its ultimate test, analogous in many ways to the laboratory experiment mentioned above. For defeat exposes all of the hidden weaknesses (erroneous theories, wrong decisions, faulty organization, the inadequacies of personnel and equipment, for example). In victory, many of these same weaknesses go unnoticed or, at best, seem insignificant.

The present study examines the Luftwaffe's defeat and indicates its major causes, the so-called "turning points." The study's conclusions represent some of the more significant findings of the GAF Monograph Project. As additional project studies are published, the interested reader will be able to study these "turning points" singly and in great detail.

Titles of supporting documents cited in the footnotes to this study are given in both German and English, followed, when applicable, by a file folder designation to enable the interested reader to locate the supporting documents and related materials in the Karlsruhe Document Collection. Following the general practice, German military ranks above colonel have not been translated. At the end of this study is a table giving equivalent German and American general officer ranks.

Both the editor and the translator of this study have sought to preserve the author's opinion and his way of stating it. The publication of this study by the United States Air Force, therefore, does not indicate USAF approval or disapproval of its contents.

ABOUT THE AUTHOR

Dr. Richard Suchenwirth, a well-known and somewhat controversial German and Austrian historian, author, teacher and lecturer, was born in Vienna on 8 October 1896. Until 1934 he pursued the career of teacher in his native Austria. In 1936 he became a citizen of Germany and, from 1936 until 1944 he was director of the Teachers' College of Munich-Pasing. In the final year of World War II he was a professor at the University of Munich. Europas letzte Stunde? (Europe's Last Hour?), the most recent of Dr. Suchenwirth's many books, was published in 1951.

Dr. Suchenwirth's interest in military history dates back to his childhood when he memorized accounts of Hannibal's battles and traced the general's campaigns on his father's maps. A lieutenant in World War I, he served as an aide to an Austrian general and learned much at firsthand concerning the problems of leadership.

In the last ten years Dr. Suchenwirth has probably interviewed more of the highest ranking German officers of World War II than any other historian. He has enjoyed a particularly close association with all of the contributors to the GAF Monograph Project and is thoroughly familiar both with their work for the project and with the documents in the Karlsruhe Document Collection.

In his own words, Dr. Suchenwirth's interest in military history ". . . lies not in any affection for militarism, but rather in the realization of the extent to which freedom and the greatness and fate of a people are dependent on military decisions; of how many human lives, how many brave soldiers and people behind the front are affected by good or bad leadership in time of war."

INTRODUCTION

The turning point of a war is that certain point at which a decisive change occurs. This change may be for the better; or it may be for the worse, pointing the way to defeat. In the case of Germany in World War II, the turning point marked a change for the worse and led inexorably from victory to defeat. In the beginning, Germany's blitzkrieg attacks moved the world to astonishment and horror, as did her rapid march to conquer nearly all of western Europe and the Balkan peninsula. Then came a turning point, which deflected the Luftwaffe (as that service with which we are most concerned here) from its triumphs and set it on the downward path to defeat and final disaster.

It may seem at first glance to denote a superficial point of view to wish to make the course of the titanic battles of World War II hang upon isolated events, decisions, or sins of omission; in short, to see in these things turning points capable of changing the course of history. Yet it cannot be denied that after a certain point (Stalingrad in the eastern theater of operations and El Alamein in the African theater) Lady Luck simply refused to smile on Germany's efforts any longer. Even battles like the one at Salerno or the attack launched by the Army Division Kempf against the enemy's southern flank at Kursk,* actions which--by all standard criteria--should have resulted in German victories, ended in defeat. There is a certain intangible factor characteristic of many turning points of war, best described perhaps as "being abandoned by the gods of military fortune."

So much, then, in justification for our treating a single event as a turning point! We must not forget, of course, that such an event rarely occurs "by accident." It is rather that some seemingly insignificant factor inherent in the event itself assumes sudden and visible importance, that some latent aspect begins to assert effects which then result in a turning point.

Latent factors of this sort, often lying far back in time and frequently dictated by considerations having no obvious connection with the event itself, may be divided into two groups. The first includes apparently remote circumstances, which at first glance would seem to have little or no direct connection with the event. These are like seeds; once the conditions are right for their germination, they can

---

*Editor's Note: Operation Citadelle (July 1943) the last, large-scale German offensive in Russia. For an account, see Erich von Manstein Lost Victories (Chicago, 1958) pp. 443 ff.

develop with frightening rapidity. To return to our original premise
of a turning point in war, as long as the military situation is favorable
and the war itself a brief one, these latent factors usually have
no opportunity to assert their effectiveness; at most they may be apparent
as annoying but insignificant trivialities. Once events have become
critical, however, their damaging effects may well reach previously
undreamed-of proportions. Inevitably they intensify the influence of
miscalculations and errors in judgement (which, of course, can never be
ruled out completely) and thereby permit unfortunate situations to
develop into turning points to disaster.

The second group includes factors whose connection with the event
is more immediately apparent. These are such things as decisions,
stubborn adherence to preconceived notions, personnel assignments,
tangible instances of neglect, and obvious sins of omission. If these
factors are of sufficient importance, they are quite capable of leading
to a turning point in the fortunes of war.

Obviously, in addition to factors such as the ones described above,
events on the field of battle,* with their frequently heroic aspects,
must be accorded their traditional role! Failure to do so would be
tantamount to denying the possibility of freedom of action and to reducing
the art of war to a mathematical equation. Even so, such detrimental
factors as inadequate leadership, the availability--or, more
important, unavailability--of the means of waging war (number of aircraft,
readiness to take new developments into account, etc.), and the
failure to carry out certain operations (as, for example, failure to
mount a strategic air war against an enemy having a high potential for
war production) are bound to place serious limitations on the chances
of success of even the most determinedly eager troops, particularly in
a war of long duration.

One other factor deserves mention here, although its detailed treatment
can be undertaken only after additional research into the matter.
Germany's capitulation in 1945, unconditional surrender at a moment when
the enemy had occupied nearly all of Germany with his troops and when
all that was left of German resistance had been pushed back into a
narrow strip of enemy-free territory to await the annihilation which
could be no more than days away, represents a total collapse uncommon
in military history. In its scope it recalls the capitulation of
Athens at the end of the Second Peloponnesian War, when only the wise
generosity of the majority of the city states waging war against her
prevented the total destruction demanded by her more fanatical enemies.
Carthage, with no one to plead her cause, was razed to the ground by

_____

*The word is used here in the figurative sense!

xii

the Romans fifty-five years after her initial capitulation.

Thus it would seem that we ought to make a distinction between turning points resulting in a moral defeat, with subsequent peace treaties of the traditional type, and turning points which lead to total catastrophe. The latter are apt to occur when a war has been fought with fanaticism and with an all-out commitment of the available resources, and above all when the goal of the war has been the complete annihilation of the enemy. Under these circumstances, although one of the belligerents has survived a number of near-crippling blows, it may still not be able to win a peace of exhaustion.

Further examination of this difference in degree, however, would lead us too far afield from the purpose of the present study. We should be required to investigate too many other fields and to delve too deeply into past history, and this study would necessarily assume the proportions of a treatise on the political and philosophical problems of waging war and on the psychology of fanaticism.

One last point concerning the applicability of our theme to the Luftwaffe. We must distinguish between turning points in the air war and turning points in the overall war which were occasioned by the inadequacy of the Luftwaffe, by its elimination from action, or by its actual defeat on the field of battle. We must bear in mind that the factors leading to a turning point for a highly technical weapon such as an air force may have their origin several years in the past, because of the length of time needed for the development of air armament (the time lapse between the development and production of aircraft engines and fuselages, for example). Thus, error of judgment in the selection of aircraft models, even when they are clearly recognized as errors, are bound to have far-reaching effects which cannot be counteracted in a short time. Because of this, factors engendered far in the past can play a much more important role in bringing about a turning point for an Air Force than would be the case for an Army.

Chapter 1

THE ORIGINS OF THE LUFTWAFFE'S DEFEAT

I - Given Factors within the Leadership of the Luftwaffe

If factors cannot be altered, they assume the proportions of fate.
If I have only a certain sum of money, for example, I cannot use it to
buy something which costs three times as much, even if my life depends
upon it. Similarly, if a man is born blind, one cannot expect him to
have a clear concept of the phenomena of color and artistic form.

The human being himself represents one such unalterable, and therefore "fate-ful" factor. He is like the leopard who cannot change his
spots no matter how much he would like to have the stripes of a tiger!
The inclinations and talents inherited by each individual, molded by
the training he receives during his formative years or by the traditional mores of his chosen profession, are determining factors throughout his life. For this reason it is tremendously difficult, if not
impossible, to guide men into directions opposed to their own inclinations, to expect them to perform tasks they have never learned, or,
once they have formed a clear opinion of their own, to try to convince
them of the rightness of someone else's opinion.

Every human institution has to cope with factors such as the above,
and the greater the scope and the responsibility of the institution,
the greater their chances of exerting a lasting influence.

The Luftwaffe had more than its share of human factors to cope
with, far more than the other two service branches. It lacked completely the decades of formative experience which had created a certain type of individual for the Army, for example. The Luftwaffe had
to be called into being almost overnight, and it had to be built from
scratch. The top-level organization formed during World War I--not
very large to begin with--had disintegrated completely. And the new
group of leaders entrusted with the build-up of Germany's air force
lacked that sense of tradition which develops automatically with long
service in a particular branch. Reichsmarschall Hermann Goering,
Generalfeldmarschall Erhard Milch, and--later on--Generaloberst Ernst
Udet were originally assigned to their Luftwaffe posts on an almost
provisional basis. It is true, of course, that those officers transferring from the Army (Generalleutnant Walther Wever, Generalfeldmarschall Albert Kesselring, Generaloberst Hans Stumpff, and General
der Flieger Karl Kitzinger) brought certain traditional attitudes with

them; even so, service on the Luftwaffe staff was something quite new for all of them, and they had much to learn about flying and aviation in general before they could become fully effective.

It is clear that the fate of the Luftwaffe was inextricably interwoven with the personal qualifications and backgrounds of these men, who were placed in charge of it with little or no preparation at a time when it was not even an independent service, at a time, in fact, when all preparations for an air arm had to be carried out in strictest secrecy. We are most immediately concerned with the men in the two highest posts, Reichs Air Minister Goering and his deputy, State Secretary Milch. Both had retired from military service when the old German air force was disbanded at the end of World War I. Then, after fourteen years of bourgeois life, they found themselves suddenly in charge of their old service. Obviously, both lacked the middle phase of military experience, the long years between captain and colonel.

Goering,[1] as the man wielding the greatest authority and bearing the chief responsibility, had an unqualified supporter in Hitler himself, who even designated him as his successor at one time. Although Goering was almost continally at loggerheads (largely through his own fault) with the chiefs of the other two services (the Commanders in Chief of the Army and Navy), although he was subjected to bitter criticism within his own service as the war progressed (especially as enemy air attacks on the German homeland became more and more successful), and although his prestige within the Party decreased steadily, his personal status remained unassailable almost to the very end, thanks to Hitler's stubborn intervention in his behalf. It was not until the last few days of the war that Hitler, believing himself betrayed by Goering, abandoned him to his fate.

Even Milch,[2] whose position was far weaker than Goering's, managed to maintain himself for seven years (1937-1944) in the face of an almost unanimously hostile front of general staff officers.

Both of these men, then, retained their roles as "inalterable factors" for the Luftwaffe until almost the very end, and the various facets of their individual personalities had much to do with determining the fate of the new service branch. The degree of authority wielded by the leaders of the Luftwaffe corresponded more closely to the authoritarian concepts of the Third Reich than did that in either of the other two services, and because of this their personal idiosyncrasies could exert a far greater influence than would have been possible within the firmly-defined, more broadly-based, and deeply traditional structure of the Army and its General Staff.

2

Over and above the rest of the personalities whose influence made itself felt within the Luftwaffe was the figure of Hitler himself, whose personal influence on the top-level air leaders was tremendous. Though enormously important, the role he played does not lend itself to objective definition; yet we must take it into account as one of the factors contributing to the final defeat of the Luftwaffe if we are to understand the full implications of the small, individual turning points which preceded it.

A. The Personalities in the Top-Level Positions

Almost until the last day of the Luftwaffe's existence, Hermann Goering was its Commander in Chief. More than any other man, he embodied its fate.

It was Goering's personality--forceful, supremely self-confident, and energetic--which determined the development of the Luftwaffe, particularly during the early days of its organization. But Goering had something of the usurper about him; this tendency to arrogate everything to himself may have been intensified by the collapse of the old imperial order in Germany, and the egotistical and selfish aspects of his nature thus had been permitted to gain greater ascendency than might otherwise have been the case. At any rate, in his innermost being he recognized only one authority--Adolf Hitler. Goering's incredible egotism was clearly a serious and dangerous drawback in a man entrusted with the fate of an entire service. Because of it, he tended to take everything personally. This, in turn, made it impossible for him to view things objectively or to face potential dangers and take the necessary precautionary measures against them. In addition, Goering's effectiveness was later impaired by a growing lassitude, occasioned in part by failing health, and an unwillingness to devote serious thought to the problems faced by the Luftwaffe. As a result, this man, whose ruthless energy and innate forcefulness of character had inspired the early build-up of the Luftwaffe and impregnated it with his own personality, was later subject to long periods of indifference during which he neglected it completely. The occasional bursts of energy which led him to intervene--often with surprisingly sound suggestions dictated by his innate common sense--were neither frequent enough nor lasting enough to compensate for his neglect. He was congenitally incapable of freeing himself of such preconceived notions as his disdain for the "noncombatant" transport pilots,[3] and he must be given the lion's share of the blame for Germany's neglect of the air transport forces--an extremely important arm in modern warfare and one whose relative lack of defensive armament makes it dangerously vulnerable.

3

Nor was Goering a supervisor on whom his colleagues could rely for support in the face of heavy opposition. He made no attempt to discourage dissension and rivalry among the hierarchy of Luftwaffe leadership. On the contrary, he may have welcomed them, since a lack of unity among his closest co-workers reduced the danger of any loss in authority due to his own incompetence.

Goering's closest colleague, State Secretary Erhard Milch, was a very hard worker, untiring, efficient, and in many respects highly qualified--quite the opposite of his superior. After a certain point, however,--which we shall examine in greater detail later on--he became involved in opposition both inside and outside the Luftwaffe, and this seriously obstructed his effectiveness. Thereafter, he devoted most of his energy to maintaining his own position, as, indeed, he had every reason to do. The situation was not a very satisfactory one. Extremely ambitious, Milch was unable to get along with the General Staff Chief, Hans Jeschonnek, and finally he even began to encounter opposition from Ernst Udet, the Chief of Luftwaffe Procurement and Supply. From that moment on (1937), Goering steadily reduced the authority of his State Secretary. Because of the growing inferiority of his position and the discord and uncertainty surrounding it (all of which must have had an effect on his personality as well), Milch was no longer able to infuse his organization with that spirit of unity, singleness of purpose, and loyalty which could have transformed the Ministry and the Luftwaffe High Command into a harmonious whole, its efforts devoted not to smoothing over petty bickerings, but to the common goal of winning the war.

Milch, in his own opinion, was a soldier; military men, however, were more apt to see in him a captain of industry and a civilian; and it must be admitted that his nonmilitary brand of insolence and his penchant for rash judgments gave them some justification for this view. Moreover, their subconscious unwillingness to take his military rank seriously (and this includes his promotion to Generalfeldmarschall) did little to further the effectiveness of his work and acted as something of a drag on the efficiency of the Reichs Air Ministry and the Luftwaffe as a whole.

Generaloberst Hans Jeschonnek,[4] Chief of the Luftwaffe General Staff, was a man exceptionally well-qualified for the military profession, uncontaminated by the poor example set by his chief Hermann Goering. Unfortunately he and State Secretary Milch were bitter enemies, and Jeschonnek allowed this enmity to influence him far more than did Milch. Basically a lonely person, Jeschonnek was also unable to make friends with Udet (Chief of Luftwaffe Procurement and Supply) or even

4

with his own deputy, Quartermaster General Hans Georg von Seidel.

Jeschonnek, like his Commander in Chief, had been a fighter pilot during World War I and his attitude towards the air reconnaissance and air transport forces was one of complete indifference. Like his chief, he was a devotee of offensive air warfare and pledged himself, heart and soul, to the concept of the dive bomber, as representing individual rather than group attack from the air.

Ernst Udet[5] was the Chief of Luftwaffe Procurement and Supply, to name the fourth of the top-level personalities. Goering had prevailed upon him to take over the Technical Office, despite the fact that he was totally unfitted for such a position. When Goering then removed Udet from the State Secretary's supervision and made him directly responsible to himself, the former friendly relationship between Udet and Milch, which could have provided Udet with a badly needed source of experienced advice and technical assistance, was destroyed completely. Udet's own suspicious nature led him to a number of remarks and actions which served to reduce the friendship between the two to a cool, mutual acceptance, which, of course, was not conducive to effective cooperation.

Udet was a complete stranger to the procurement side of air armament. He was deeply interested in the niceties of development and, in his enthusiasm for this aspect of his task, tended to neglect the aspect of production. On the other hand, he seemed to be incapable of taking a firm hand in the selection of the models to be developed. He was the first of the top-level Luftwaffe leaders to go; the handwriting on the wall began to be visible with his suicide on 17 November 1941.

*   *   *

Can there be any doubt but that these personalities alone harbored the seeds of the disaster to come?

Goering was intoxicated with his authority to command regardless of whether his commands were necessary or even logical; and he was completely innocent of professional knowledge, but hampered by unreasonable prejudices which he would not relinquish. He was incapable of keeping his house in order or of imbuing his staff with a sense of common purpose. In sum, Goering's behaviour during peacetime, and to an even greater degree in wartime, offered a remarkable illustration of corruption.

State Secretary and deputy Erhard Milch, who was forced to be continually on his guard against attempts by the General Staff to

5

deprive him of power and authority, had no outlet for his ability and diligence.

Jeschonnek, as General Staff Chief, was incapable of making and sustaining friendly personal contact with his top-level colleagues within the Luftwaffe; like Goering, he clung stubbornly to preconceived prejudices.

Lastly, Udet (Chief of Luftwaffe Procurement and Supply) was unfitted for his job and extremely one-sided in his interests.

And each of these men was at odds with the other three.

Let us see if we can connect these personality factors to the events of the war itself.

In the first place, the Luftwaffe, as the weapons system destined to bear the brunt of the war, without respite from the beginning to the end, was, from its founding until its disintegration, deprived of the firmly formative spirit of a Commander in Chief sincerely concerned for the welfare of his men. Those pilots who actually got to see and talk with Goering, especially those received by him at Karinhall,* went away with a feeling of uneasiness rather than confidence. Goering's hand grew progressively weaker as the demands made upon the Luftwaffe increased. The greater the need for firm leadership, the more conspicuously was it lacking. The weakness of Goering's position was further augmented by his arrogance, which made it impossible for him to cooperate effectively with the leaders of the Army.✝ For example, when the Luftwaffe was ordered to release some of its superfluous ground organization personnel to the Army, Goering made certain that they could not be utilized to fill up the depleted divisions on the Russian front. He was determined at all costs to retain his authority over these men. As a result, they were hurriedly trained for infantry combat, in which they had had no experience whatever, and committed by unit in actions which led to their rapid and complete decimation. If they had been integrated into an experienced Army division, they could have learned their trade better and might have avoided total annihilation. As it was, Goering's stubbornness destroyed a chance to increase

----

*Editor's Note: Goering's estate on the Shorfheide, about 25 miles north of Berlin.

✝It is striking to note the unanimously scathing evaluation of Goering in the memoirs of Army officers from Hossbach to von Manstein.

the striking power of the German Army by reinforcing it with well-trained soldiers who could have replaced the heavy personnel losses in the noncommissioned officer ranks.

We could mention countless other instances in which Goering's megalomania and need for recognition led him to tragic misuse of his authority. Later on, we shall examine some of the more important of these instances in connection with our treatment of certain significant military events.

Nor can Jeschonnek be absolved of blame. His chief mistake was his stubborn refusal to see, until it was too late, the danger threatening Germany from the air and to recognize the significance of the four-engine bombers being developed by the enemy. The obstinacy which revealed itself in his inflexible faith in the dive-bomber made him insist for far too long on the development of aircraft with good diving performance. In tragic contradiction of his truly excellent military ability and his fine personal qualities, this youthful General Staff Chief precipitated the Luftwaffe into a serious crisis.

Let us next turn to Udet. It was largely his fault that Germany's air armament program was so inadequate during the fatal first years of the war. In later times the Reichsmarschall, although hardly qualified to express an opinion on the matter, denounced him bitterly for his failure.* This tragic error, for which Udet was technically responsible, was largely the result of the helplessness of this really very fine man in the face of a position for which he was not fitted. He was incapable of mastering the intrigues and rivalries which ran riot in the air armament industry; indeed, he seemed incapable of even recognizing them for what they were. A man who shrank from ruthless action, he was simply unable to keep industry in line. In addition, he lacked the ability to evaluate the capacities of his fellow-men and to surround himself with those who would be of most use to him in his work. He was deeply interested in the developmental phase of air armament and displayed unusual insight and practical originality in this field; unfortunately, he never succeeded in acquiring equal interest and understanding for

---

*"If he were alive today, I would have no alternative but to say to him: 'You are responsible for destroying the Luftwaffe!'" (Stenographische Niederschrift ueber die Besprechung am 9.10.43 auf dem Obersalzberg, Atelierhaus Speer, 15 Uhr, Geheim. (Stenographic notes of a conference held on 9 October 1943 in Studio Speer on the Obersalzberg, 15:00 hours, Secret), copy in C/IV/2a, Karlsruhe Document Collection.)

the problems of procurement.

The war was a matter of life or death for Germany. The leaders of the Luftwaffe, however, were anything but a dedicated community; not even the General Staff itself was capable of unity of purpose. And throughout the entire course of the war we find no sign of any attempt to do away with the rivalries and intrigues which were bound, in time, to poison the effectiveness of all concerned in them. Udet's suicide, which might have been avoided if he had been given the chance to function in an atmosphere of comradely loyalty, was a foregone conclusion under the existing circumstances. And his death was soon to be followed by the suicide--just as inevitable--of the lonely young General Staff Chief, Jeschonnek.

Let us consider, however, the effects which these suicides must have had upon the spirit of the Luftwaffe leaders and upon their faith in an ultimate victory. In both cases every possible step was taken to hush up the manner of death, but in both cases the truth managed to leak out. And the truth could hardly have been very encouraging.

We have no choice but to conclude that the personality factors inherent in the leadership of the Luftwaffe bore the seeds of eventual disaster.

B. The Top-Level Command Structure of the Reichs Air Ministry

It may seem strange, at this point, to examine a realm of bureaucracy and organization like the top-level command of the Luftwaffe. Unimportant as it may seem, however, it was this organization which helped to prevent the development of a true spirit of comradeship within the Luftwaffe.[6]

The Luftwaffe's top-level command adapted itself well to existing conditions until 1937/38. It is true that Goering, burdened with a plethora of other offices and duties, often had to withdraw from active participation in the affairs of the Luftwaffe--which he termed "his" service--but at such times he was very adequately represented by his permanent deputy, State Secretary Milch. At no time during its history did the Luftwaffe command organization function so smoothly and with such unity of purpose as under the aegis of Goering during his most energetic period. The death, on 3 June 1936, of Generalleutnant Walther Wever (first chief of the Luftwaffe General Staff) marked the beginning of hostilities between Milch and the Luftwaffe General Staff, the latter chafing under the solicitous interference to which Milch, as Goering's

8

permanent representative, felt himself not only entitled but obliged.

The Luftwaffe General Staff championed a kind of equality of authority to begin with, although it is likely that its ultimate goal was the exclusive right of command within its own organization, which means that the Chief of the General Staff--and not Milch--would have become Goering's permanent deputy. There was undeniably something to be said for this plan, but its realization was bound to involve a struggle with Milch, who, after all, was already in possession of the deputyship. Since there could be no thought of deposing Milch because of incompetence, and since he was by no means a man of submissive character, the struggle was inevitably a long and hard one. Goering, as Reichs Air Minister, may have interpreted the struggle between Milch and the Chief of the General Staff as no more than healthy opposition; in any case, the solution which he decided upon to end the conflict was the worst possible one, because it was no more than a half-measure; its only virtue being that it was the easiest solution and made the least trouble for Goering himself. He made the General Staff directly subordinate to himself, as he did later on with a number of Luftwaffe offices, and restricted Milch's permanent deputyship--which would have given the latter both insight into General Staff policies and a certain degree of influence over them--to those periods when he was himself absent from the Ministry.

Neither protagonist was satisfied with Goering's solution; they subsided into a relationship of grudging cooperation, and the silent struggle for top authority continued. Fearful of losing still more of his influence, Milch tried to strengthen his position by taking over first the office of the Inspector General (in 1939) and then (in 1941) the office of the Chief of Luftwaffe Procurement and Supply. His efforts were doomed to failure, however, and as the war progressed, he was forced to watch his position--both as State Secretary and as Inspector General--crumble into insignificance until 1944, when, in the words of Generaloberst Loerzer,[7] (Goering's friend and Luftwaffe Chief of Personnel from 1943 to 1944) the once all-powerful deputy was "organized out" of the Luftwaffe. With this the General Staff had finally gained its victory, but there was little cause for rejoicing, for by this time the final defeat of the Luftwaffe had already begun, and one of the factors bringing about this defeat was surely the lack of inner unity in the ranks of the Luftwaffe's top commanders.

Quite apart from the friction and uncertainty which it caused, the end effect of Goering's reorganization was to leave the Luftwaffe without a leader. For he had weakened Milch's position without increasing his own participation in Luftwaffe affairs. His old, easy life continued; in fact, as time went on, it became easier. He no longer held the reins firmly, but took hold of them gingerly and only when he happened to be in the mood.

Lack of leadership is one of the worst evils which can befall a military organization. This is just as true in peacetime, and laxity then may well give rise to wartime defeat. During wartime, lack of leadership is an almost certain guarantee of failure.

Within the Luftwaffe the lack of firm leadership spread like a slow poison. It showed in the failure to plan and--even more--to carry through systematic programs of air armament, pilot training, and personnel assignment; and it was revealed ultimately in the total lack of any consistent delineation of the role of leadership itself. For the most part, as time went on, the concept of command gradually degenerated into mere administration. No body of authority, but least of all a military one, can afford this sort of degeneration.

It was without doubt one of the factors contributing to the demise of the Luftwaffe.

C. Loyalty to Hitler - Faith in Hitler - Abject Obedience to Hitler

None of the personality factors significant to the history of the German Luftwaffe, however, played such an important role as those of a single man, Adolf Hitler, who held Germany under the fateful sway of his personal forcefulness from 1933 until 1945.

Coming from a simple background, the product of a joyless childhood and the unhappy conditions of the Vienna of his youth, the World War I private utilized the confusion resulting from the collapse of 1918 and the general dissatisfaction at the provisions of the Versailles Treaty in order to become the founder and leader of the strongest political party Germany had ever had.

In 1933 he became Reichs Chancellor and a year and a half later, at Hindenburg's death, he assumed the title of Fuehrer and Reichs Chancellor. His personal struggle for political power had become the nemesis of the Weimar Republic. After Hindenburg's death he embodied the fate of seventy million, then eighty million Germans, and finally that of Europe and the world. The collapse of his regime in 1945 did not restore the world to its prewar status.

From the very beginning, Hitler's unswerving self-confidence inspired his listeners, even those of higher social background than his own, first with a feeling of fascination and then with an unwilling conviction of his superiority. Even during the early days of his career he was accustomed to do most of the talking himself, and his "conferences" were usually monologues with the other members listening to Hitler. An uncanny power seemed to emanate from him, an almost eerie personal magnetism, and this--coupled with his truly amazing powers of memory in an era when most of his contemporaries made no attempt at all to train and develop this faculty--made it very difficult for anyone hearing his speeches and pronouncements to remain free of his influence. Only confirmed skeptics managed to escape his sway, and then only so long as they stayed well out of his sphere of influence.

For all those, however, who had followed his political activity from the beginning, he was truly the "leader." People relied implicitly on his faculty for making the right decision in any situation and believed him to be politically infallible. The conviction that he was destined to succeed in everything he undertook was deeply rooted among his followers. The antipathy felt by most of the Party leaders for the two Christian churches led to a kind of Hitler-worship reminiscent of the days of the Roman emperors. More and more rarely were opinions expressed which might in any way cast doubt upon this cult. Most opposition subsided with the overthrow, in 1932, of Gregor Strasser, who represented quite a different direction of thought as regarded domestic policy, and the last vestige of a certain independence of spirit disappeared when Ernst Roehm and his SA leaders went down in the Blood Bath of 30 June 1934.*

As far as its relationship to Hitler was concerned, the Party went through all the various stages from loyalty to the Fuehrer, with the emotional element of faith and devotion as its guiding principle in

---

*Editor's Note: Ernst Roehm, Chief of the SA (Sturm Abteilung)-- the Nazi Party's instrument of violence for the execution of special, extralegal tasks--constituted a threat to Hitler for two reasons; he was ambitious and powerful. His ambition was to become a sort of super defense minister over the Armed Forces, the SA, the police, etc. Thus Roehm embarrassed Hitler in his relations with the Army, whose support Hitler badly needed. Roehm and his followers were executed on Hitler's order in a series of raids organized and led by Goering and Himmler. Gregor Strasser, although no longer a direct threat to Hitler, had offered serious opposition in the past and thus, on the occasion of this SA purge, Strasser became a sort of "target of opportunity" and was murdered along with a number of other people in the same category. See Alan Bullock, Hitler, A Study in Tyranny, (New York, 1952) pp. 258-279 passim.

the political struggle, through faith in the Fuehrer, embodying the conviction that Hitler was the saviour sent by God (Providence or Fate) to assuage Germany's economic and social ills and to liberate her from foreign domination, and finally to absolute obedience to the Fuehrer, with its concomitant suppression of all independent thought and personal doubt. The motto "Fuehrer, command and we shall follow!", repeated again and again by organized choruses at political rallies, on placards, and on banners, acted as hypnotic suggestion on Germany's masses as they went into action with all the inexorableness of a religious movement.

Hermann Goering was one of Hitler's earliest followers. We know the later Reichsmarschall best as an arrogant egotist whose vanity concealed ruthless ambition and a good deal of disdain for his fellow-men. Even so, in contradiction to the opinion held by Grossadmiral a. D. Raeder, one of Goering's severest critics, there would seem to be no doubt concerning Goering's loyalty to Hitler. We may also be certain that he had a great deal of faith in the Fuehrer and that he considered him to be the chosen saviour of the German nation. His first wife was devoted to Hitler with an almost adolescent adoration. Then, too, Goering was fully aware of his indebtedness to his Fuehrer for the power, prestige, and income which he enjoyed. This probably became even more painfully clear to him later on, when his influence with Hitler was on the wane. In the beginning, however, there was no thought of "abject obedience to the Fuehrer" as far as Goering was concerned. Hitler often turned to him for advice, and he was easily the first in line after him. It was Goering's intervention, for example, which moved Hitler, in March 1938, to more rapid action than he had planned in the question of Austria. In March 1939, Goering tried to dissuade his chief from establishing the Protectorate of Bohemia-Moravia,* and prior to the outbreak of the war he took it upon himself to utilize the offices of a Swedish go-between, Birger Dahlerus, to preserve peace at all costs. In other words, Goering still had a mind of his own and a certain amount of initiative as a private citizen. It was not until after the war began, as the problems faced by the Luftwaffe became more and more critical and as it began to be obvious that the Luftwaffe

---

*Editor's Note: The dissolution of Czechoslovakia, which began after the Munich Conference (29-30 Sept 1938) with the German military occupation of the Sudetenland and its subsequent annexation, reached its culmination six months later (March 1939) with the establishment of the German Protectorate of Bohemia-Moravia and the German recognition of Slovakian independence. The defense of Slovakia, in turn, became a German responsibility.

could not possibly master the tasks heaped upon it--approximately in
June of 1942--that Goering joined the ranks of those whose obedience to
the Fuehrer was automatic and indiscriminating. His motives in doing
so were not very idealistic. Above all, he wanted to regain Hitler's
confidence, which had cooled noticeably since the Luftwaffe had begun
to suffer defeat, and in order to do so he gave up all pretense of
independence. Soon, however, he was motivated by fear--fear for his
own skin, fear of being deposed, fear of being pushed into the background during his conferences at the Fuehrer's headquarters by Martin
Bormann, head of the Nazi Party, who was growing more and more powerful. His fear expressed itself in a fierce jealousy of his General
Staff Chief, Hans Jeschonnek,* long a favorite of Hitler's. Goering
did everything he could think of to demonstrate his undivided allegiance
to the Fuehrer, even to the extent of giving him absolute obedience.
Under these circumstances it is perhaps all the more comprehensible
that he made such a violent and desperate effort to succeed Hitler
when General der Flieger Karl Koller told him of Hitler's collapse on
23 April 1945 and urged him to step into the breach.† Hitler's reaction
to Goering's attempt was no less violent, and in an outburst of bitterness, disappointment, and contempt he issued hasty orders to arrest
the Reichsmarschall and even threatened to have him shot.

The motives leading to Jeschonnek's faith in Hitler and his frequently unreasoning obedience to him[8] were far more idealistic. His
experience, as a youthful volunteer during World War I and later as an
officer deeply depressed by the conditions in his fatherland, made him
unhesitatingly ready to pledge his loyalty to Hitler, the Messiah of
a new and better order. His faith in Hitler's genius was genuine. He
was sure that if Hitler could prevent a war in 1938, he would be capable
of doing so in 1939. At the time the war broke out, his faith was still
unshaken. His attitude was one of inflexible confidence in the inevi-
tability of a German victory and, as late as the winter of 1941, he
still refused to listen to the "almost traitorous" doubts which Quartermaster General von Seidel began to put before him. Not until Stalingrad
did he begin to doubt that the outcome of the war would be favorable
for Germany, but once he opened his mind to these doubts, they rapidly

---

*Goering once said to him: "You always stand there like a lieuten-
ant with your hands at your trouser seams when you talk with Hitler!"
(Reported to the author by General der Flieger a. D. Rudolf Meister,
on 27 January 1955).

†Editor's Note: "Successor to the Fuehrer" was a recognized part
of Goering's full title.

developed into certainties. From this point on, he was no longer indiscriminating in his obedience to Hitler. His veneration of Hitler as a
person presumably remained unchanged; by this time he had long since
lost any respect he may have had for Goering. It is quite possible
that his suicide, which may really have been a last, desperate gesture
of protest against Goering and his tragically incompetent leadership,
was also an expression of the despair, loneliness, and hopelessness
which Hitler was no longer able to dispel.

In the case of State Secretary Milch, we can hardly speak of uncritical obedience to Hitler; Milch was not the sort of man to give
unquestioning obedience to anyone. Even so, Seidel speaks of him as
"personally deeply loyal to Hitler."[9] The enthusiasm and energy with
which Milch, who was on excellent terms with the Party and its leaders,
worked to realize Hitler's goal of a strong German air force could only
serve to strengthen the faith of his co-workers in their Supreme Commander.

We must be clear about one thing. The Luftwaffe, a newly created
service with a far higher percentage of younger men than the other two
branches, was inevitably more receptive to Hitler and National Social-
ism than the Army. The Luftwaffe was not bound by tradition; there was
no leader caste of Prussian nobility, insistent on its right to rule.*
During the period of the Weimar Republic, the Army had established a
little-publicized but very real position of power and felt itself to be
above the machinations of a political party.[10] The newly created Luftwaffe, on the other hand, was commanded by Hitler's closest associate,
who had no scruples about using his personal prestige to increase the
funds, recognition, and degree of loyalty accorded to his service
branch by the new state. There is no point in denying the fact that
Goering--whose energy and effectiveness during the early years of the
Luftwaffe's existence are still recognized and appreciated today, even
by Luftwaffe men who never fell under his personal sway--had a great
deal of influence, particularly on people who were so casually asso-
ciated with him that they could afford to be indulgent as regards his
weaknesses. Of those staff officers transferred from the Army, the

_____

*None of the older staff officers taken over from the Army was a
member of the nobility. The only ones in the Luftwaffe command hierarchy were Freiherren (Barons) von Richthofen, von Waldau, von Seidel,
and the last Quartermaster General von Criegern. Generalfeldmarschall
Ritter von Greim, of the postwar Bavarian nobility, had been knighted
by Max Josef for his service during World War I. But how little these
names mean when we compare them with the Army list!

most significant was Generalleutnant Wever, whose memory is still alive today in German Air Force circles. Wever, to put it mildly, was receptive to Hitler and his ideas, although there is only one source[11] for the statement attributed to him (shortly before his promotion to the rank of General) to the effect that the Luftwaffe officer corps would either be National Socialist or it wouldn't be at all!

Wever's activity with the Luftwaffe was cut so short by his death that he experienced only the favorable aspects of Germany's new government; he was spared the necessity of coping with the unfavorable ones. There can be no doubt but that he saw in the Luftwaffe a sword destined to strike a powerful blow for the future of Germany. He faced the prospect of war with his typical manly confidence.

The second of the officers taken over from the Army, Colonel--and soon thereafter General--Albert Kesselring, was a thoroughly idealistic person, an inveterate optimist willing to fight for his convictions. Kesselring took over his new position with all the enthusiasm of his temperamental nature and soon gave evidence of his gift for winning over his colleagues and of his untiring perseverance, qualities which characterized his military career. Promoted to Generalfeldmarschall by Hitler during World War II, Kesselring never permitted his faith in the Fuehrer to waver, and retained Hitler's full confidence until the end.

The third Army officer to achieve a position of prominence in the Luftwaffe was Generaloberst Hans Juergen Stumpff, a man of docile temperament, glad to be able to follow the strong voice of authority. Even Stumpff, however, was caught up by the vitality emanating from the new government and from his immediate chief, Goering.

These, then, were the older staff officers who transferred to the Luftwaffe from the Reichswehr.* A second group comprised Reichswehr officers who had been active in the former German air force or had subsequently received flight training at Lipetsk./ On the average, this group was about ten years younger than the aforementioned, and brought with it a certain youthful eagerness and optimism which was easily

---

*Editor's Note: The German National Defense Establishment under the Versailles Treaty.

/Editor's Note: A Russian base at which German pilots were secretly given combat flight training (1925-1933).

attracted to a government dedicated to action and progress.[12] All the others, the older "pour le merite" wearers from Keller to Osterkamp, were also fired by the enthusiastic activity of the early days. Ritter von Greim, the most serious-minded of the latter group and easily the most significant personality among them, was the victim of a positively abject devotion to Hitler until the very end. On 20 May 1945, the Fuehrer and his empire having finally succumbed to the long-threatening shadow of death and destruction, von Greim, unable to face the future, took his own life.*

The course of events since 1933 clearly lends credence to the hypothesis that the Luftwaffe, augmenting its members year by year with especially selected younger men eager for action, felt its existence to be closely tied to Hitler and his political fate.

And how many successes Hitler had to his credit! --the suppression of all active opposition at home; the revitalization of German industry and the abolishment of unemployment, which had haunted the Weimar Republic since its inception; the confirmation of Germany's freedom of action by walking out on the League of Nations (14 October 1933); the nonaggression pact with Poland (26 January 1934); the halting of the

---

*In that section of his diary covering the "last month" (14 April to 27 May 1945), (Der letzte Monat, Munich, 1949), Karl Koller, the last Chief of the Luftwaffe General Staff, reports a telephone conversation with von Greim, who had just been appointed Feldmarschall to replace Goering (by then persona non grata). When Koller commented, "Our association will be a very short one. We can do nothing more with the Luftwaffe - the end is in sight," von Greim replied: "Just wait a bit - don't lose faith! Everything will turn out all right. I feel much strengthened after my sojourn with the Fuehrer; his tremendous power has been a fountain of youth for me. The Fuehrer sat at my bedside /von Greim was recovering from a wound/ and discussed matters with me. He took back everything he said about the Luftwaffe; all his reproaches were directed at Goering alone. As far as the Luftwaffe itself is concerned, he had only the highest praise; he knows exactly what we have accomplished. His words were a source of gratification to me." Koller, a down-to-earth, realistic Bavarian, adds: "Fountain of youth - good Lord, this is like an insane asylum! What is the matter with me that I can't follow the flights of fancy of these people and can't for the life of me see the 'way out' which they prophecy? Do they have a sixth sense that enables them to see things which I, as a normal mortal, am unable to see? That can't be it! Yet there are so many things today that make me doubt the conclusions of my own common sense!"

16

encircling Stresa Front;* the naval agreement with England (June 1935); the return of the Saar (January 1935); the introduction of conscription and the revelation of German rearmament (March 1935); and the deployment of troops to the Rhineland (March 1936), although the Versailles Treaty had clearly specified that no German troops might be stationed there. And Hitler's greatest coups in foreign policy, the annexation of Austria (13 March 1938) and the absorption of the Sudeten Land, succeeded in spite of the serious reservations held by the Chief of the Army General Staff, General Ludwig Beck. Despite the memorandums warning against action in the Sudeten Land which he issued under dates of 5 and 29 May, 3 June, 16 and 29 July 1938,⌿ Beck was unable to disguise completely his inner adherence to Hitler's views, which were bound to lead, sooner or later, to the dissolution of Czechoslovakia and, thereby, to war. The Conference at Munich (September 1938) showed Hitler at the most powerful moment of his entire career, at a point at which he had violated both the letter and the spirit of the Versailles Treaty and had succeeded in obtaining not only Italian, but also English and French, consent for his action. In March 1939, the reincorporation of the Memel Land⌿ and the dissolution of Czechoslovakia (establishment of the Protectorate Bohemia/Moravia and assumption of protective sovereignty over Slovakia) cost him little more than a flick of the wrist. This first step in the direction of German self-determination, at the same time a step in the direction of final disaster, seemed to the

---

*Editor's Note: The so-called Stresa Front grew out of a conference between Great Britain, France and Italy held in Stresa (April 1935) as a protest to German rearmament. The solidarity of the Stresa Front was broken the following June when Great Britain, without consulting Italy or France, concluded a naval agreement with Germany which allowed Germany to rebuild her fleet to 35% of the strength of the British Fleet.

⌿In his memorandum of 29 May 1938, Beck warns against underestimating the military strength of France and England when he says: "Moreover, it is obvious that Germany, either alone or allied with Italy, is hardly in a position to meet France and England on the field of battle." Wolfgang Foerster, Ein General kaempft gegen den Krieg (A General Fights against War), based on the papers of General Staff Chief Ludwig Beck, (Munich, 1949), p. 92; the underlining is Foerster's.

⌿Editor's Note: Memel, an old Hanseatic port on the Baltic, was administered by the League of Nations following World War I. In 1924 it was ceded to Lithuania, only to be returned to Germany following a German ultimatum on 22 March 1939.

world to be further evidence of Hitler's innate talent for success. Even during the early days of the war, Hitler's prophecy of the military weakness of France seemed destined to triumph over Beck's cautiously high estimate of the fighting effectiveness and strength of the French Army, as Germany easily conquered France in a rapid and brilliant campaign. It was at this time that the phrase "the greatest military leader of all times" was minted, and it soon found its way into common usage.

Thus far Hitler's intuition, his appraisal of the enemy, and his stubborn will seemed to have been right. Adulation of this sort for a single individual, however, was to prove a source of serious danger.

"No man may be said to have been happy until his death." These words of the Athenian sage, Solon, reported to us by Herodotus, have sounded their warning throughout the history of the world. Their meaning can be extended, too; before his death, no man may be said to have been invincible, to have been intuitively right all of the time, in short, to have been destined to succeed in everything to which he turned his hand.

Let us see what effects this boundless faith in one man, this irrational belief in his divine power, had on the top-level leaders of the Luftwaffe. We cannot deny that it served as a source of inspiration and enthusiasm in the beginning. Both Goering and Jeschonnek, whom the wave of Hitler's success carried to the peaks of their respective careers (Goering to the unique rank of Reichsmarschall and Jeschonnek, in 1939 still a lieutenant colonel, to the ranks of General der Flieger and finally, in 1943, of Generaloberst), felt themselves to be the architects of Germany's liberation; the chosen instruments of the greatest military leader of all times, as they thought. They were highly gratified to be able to contribute, with their Luftwaffe, to the final victory, and they were ready to prove themselves worthy of their chief by committing Luftwaffe strength to the limit, with a growing disregard for sound military planning. Doubts, arguments of logic, and difficulties were simply beside the point in view of the magnitude of their mission.

Neither one, however, (and this was true to a greater or lesser degree of all those under Hitler's sway--the degree depending upon the extent to which they believed in him) was a free man any longer. Neither was capable of using his mind dispassionately. They were no longer the guiding spirits of their service branch, able to evaluate its position in the light of the overall situation and to make the appropriate decisions coolly and objectively. Not true of an established monarchy, basing its existence on inherited tradition or

18

parliamentary law, it is the curse of the totalitarian state that critical thinking is interpreted as heresy, doubt, and defeatism. This is inevitable because the head of a totalitarian state must base his strength on general acceptance of his program--even if this acceptance must be forced--in order to maintain and increase his power. Goering, with his growing inclination towards a pasha-like manner of living-- not necessarily an evil in itself--, and Jeschonnek, with his unswerving confidence in victory and his isolation from his colleagues, were both slaves, balancing themselves between Fuehrer and Fatherland on a narrow and perilous tightrope.

Both had already been the victims of a number of delusions. Was the Hitler of 1940/41 the same as the Hitler of 1938/39, when all of his prophecies came true? Had not the British declared war--in spite of Hitler's prophecy to the contrary? And had not they persuaded the French to help them? Had Hitler succeeded in making peace with England, as he intended to do after the campaign in Poland or, at the latest, after the German victory in France? And--assuming that he had no other choice in the matter but to march against Russia--was the Soviet campaign really turning out to be the fast one he had expected and, indeed, prophecied?[13]

There is no such thing as infallibility in military or political life, and those who are spared the ignominy of defeat are rare favorites of fate. Anyone who pledges himself wholly to a leader in the assumption that the latter has always been right and will always continue to be right automatically takes leave of his own freedom of judgment and becomes nothing more than an instrument of another's will, regardless of how high his position may be.

Constant subordination to a superior personality, no matter how admirable a one, must lead sooner or later to atrophy of the individual's ability to think for himself. And one of the basic premises for the successful leadership of a military service during wartime must surely remain the ability of its commander in chief and general staff chief to think independently and to draw the appropriate conclusions from their thinking.

This is not only indispensible for the service branch concerned, but also for the commander in chief and general staff chief themselves. In the case of the Luftwaffe, the primary mission--primary to the exclusion of all else--of both of these personalities was to carry out the will of the Fuehrer they thought to be infallible. And therein lay the greatest danger for the future.

II - Areas of Neglect and Error before the War

During the Luftwaffe's short period of existence, its General Staff, which was not created until 1 August 1936, had accomplished a prodigious amount of work. We must not ignore the fact that the Luftwaffe, despite only six--actually only four--peacetime years in which to prepare itself, played a decisive role in the campaigns in Poland, France, and the Balkans, and in the occupation of Crete, and also made it possible for Germany to attain her initial successes in Russia before the advent of winter.

Nevertheless, when the impetus of the German offensive in Russia began to slow down and the original blitz campaign turned into a war of long duration, the inadequacy of peacetime planning began to make itself felt. And this inadequacy, for the most part, could be traced directly to oversights and errors on the part of the General Staff.

A. Training - the Step-Child of the Luftwaffe [14]

When the top-level command of the Luftwaffe was reorganized on 1 February 1939, Branch 3 (Training) was restricted to tactical training in an effort to perfect the striking power of the new force. Pilot training and time-consuming individual training programs were turned over to the newly created office of the Chief of Training, who was subordinate to the State Secretary and Inspector General of the Luftwaffe. With this division of labor, the General Staff controlled the training of the immediately available personnel; not, however, of the personnel in depth. From the latter source, of course, come the reserves most needed in the midst of war.

There can be no doubt of the fact that the restrictions placed on Branch 3 originated in great part with the man who became Chief of the Luftwaffe General Staff on 1 February 1939. Hans Jeschonnek, the fourth and easily the most significant of the Luftwaffe General Staff Chiefs, placed very little value on the development of a closely-knit training program. His interests lay in other directions. He was a man of his own day. His responses to the demands of his time were appropriate and sure, and he even showed a certain talent for improvisation when necessary. The establishment of a systematic program of training, by its very nature time-consuming and directed to the future, interested him far less than the employment of already available forces, in other words, of the strategic-tactical force in being. This occupied his interest to the exclusion of almost everything else.

And this attitude of his, although incidentally coinciding with his personal make-up and inclinations, was based primarily on his

20

unshakable conviction of the proper way for the Reich to conduct a potential war. In his opinion, Germany was capable of conducting successfully only a short, limited war. In order to do this, she would have to commit all of her forces, including reserves, at the very beginning. The enemy must be overrun by a blitz campaign before he had a chance to make full use of his potential strength.[15]

This was clearly an oversimplification of Hitler's own views. In the event of a war with the western powers England and France, Hitler had spoken of a war to the end, and had warned that the leaders of state might have to be prepared for a struggle of ten to fifteen years' duration.[16]

Undeniably there was a certain element of truth in Jeschonnek's opinions. The concept of a blitz campaign inevitably calls for the immediate commitment of such overwhelming strength that all enemy resistance is nipped in the bud. And Germany's campaigns in Poland and in the Balkans were actually classic examples of an avalanche-like employment of superior strength. During the campaign in France, the numerical superiority of the German Luftwaffe assured a relatively quick victory and, as a matter of fact, moved the British to keep their Spitfires at home in self-defense and to utilize them only sporadically over Dunkirk in rescue actions in behalf of the British Expeditionary Force.

These same principles of concentration on the force in being and commitment of all available strength, however, were bound to be unsatisfactory as soon as the time factor became important, i.e. as soon as it became apparent that the enemy could not be subdued within a matter of days or weeks, but would have time to recover and to build up his own air armament.

In other words, to use an expression more strictly applicable to World War I, the situation changed as soon as the mobile war turned into a war of position. It is true, of course, that only geographically extensive nations such as Russia or America could indulge in this type of warfare indefinitely. Even so, the British Isles managed to maintain itself in the face of German blitz attacks during the summer and fall of 1940. It turned out to be impossible for the Luftwaffe to gain air supremacy over Britain or even to deliver blows sufficiently crippling to put her out of action for any length of time.

*   *   *

The Luftwaffe General Staff had more or less completely given up any claim to influence over the training program in 1939. The creation

21

of the new office of the Chief of Training, however, was hardly a suitable substitute in case of war, especially in view of its extreme decentralization. The Chief of Training himself had no direct supervision over the training program. The Pilot Training Commanders were subordinate to the Air Fleet Commands, which meant that the latter had direct control over the schools and training equipment. In the last analysis, the training program was under the supervision of what we might term all-powerful step-fathers, who naturally were far more concerned with immediate fighting preparedness than with the pampering of a training program whose effects could not be felt right away.

When the war began, the air fleet commanders in chief, no doubt having discussed the matter thoroughly with one another, began their ruthless raid on the schools to requisition Ju-52's* (for use as transport aircraft) as well as other types of training aircraft (for use as courier planes). In this way the Chief of Training lost not only the Ju-52's for the C-schools /advanced flying schools of the Luftwaffe7 and instrument flight schools, but also their crews, made up of highly trained instructional personnel. It was not until much later that aircraft and crews found their way back to him, and even then in nothing like their full numbers. Finally, the Chief of Training succeeded in persuading the Commander in Chief of the Luftwaffe that the air fleet commanders should have nothing to do with training as long as the war continued.

And with all this, it must be remembered that from the beginning, the base of the Luftwaffe training program had not been very broad. At the time the office of the Chief of Training was set up, there were

_____

*Editor's Note: The Ju (Junkers) 52, a three-engine, low-wing, transport monoplane, was used by the Luftwaffe from the beginning of the Spanish Civil War until the end of World War II. It was Germany's standard, transport aircraft.

/"The pilot training schools (elementary flight schools, instrument flight schools, and air academies) at Germany's disposal were too few to compensate for the losses in pilot personnel and to meet the personnel requirements for the activation of new units. It was out of the question to attempt to build up a pilot reserve." (General der Flieger a. D. Paul Deichmann's contribution to the study, Die Ausbildung der deutschen Luftwaffe bis zum Kriegsbeginn (Training of the Luftwaffe up to the Beginning of the War), B/III/1a, Karlsruhe Document Collection. See also B/I, B/II, B/III, Karlsruhe Document Collection, for reports concerning the interference of the air fleet commanders in the Luftwaffe training program.)

only three bomber schools, one naval aviation school, and--fantastic though it seems--only one fighter school. General der Flieger a. D. Paul Deichmann, former Chief of Staff of the Chief of Training, writes as follows: "In early 1939, when the office was first created, the Chief of Training prepared a report for the Chief of the General Staff and requested authorization for new pilot training schools. The General Staff refused his request, stating that all technical resources were being wholly utilized in the activation of new front units."17

Immediately after taking office, the Chief of Training tried to improve the situation by parcelling out training assignments to the active units, which did have access to training aircraft at their assigned air fields. Even so, there was then and remained a serious discrepancy between the need for training, as evaluated by the Chief of Training, and the facilities available for training. There could be no thought of building up a trained reserve.*

It was no secret that a good fighter pilot needed one year of training, and a bomber crew as much as two years. These facts should have served as a warning in the event of war.

One question remains unanswered. After the Munich conference, Hitler, impressed by the scope of Britain's armament program, ordered an immediate reinforcement of Luftwaffe strength--almost a fivefold increase. His order was quite logical, for two reasons. In the first place, England's all-out armament program was certainly an indication of the fact that Europe was not fully satisfied by the outcome of the Munich conference. On the contrary, one of the strongest participants in the Munich pact thought it necessary to build up her military pre-paredness. And such an act could be directed only against Germany; thus, it was a clear indication of the political atmosphere. If Hitler was to maintain Germany's military superiority, i.e. the basis for the bloodless victories he had enjoyed so far, the only way he could meet the British bid was by producing an even higher card. However, the superiority of Germany's modern air force was already the highest card

---

*The effects began to manifest themselves in January 1941, when German losses suffered in the air battle against Britain began to increase steadily. The reports issued by the Quartermaster General of the Luftwaffe for this period repeatedly emphasize the lack of crews capable of operating the Ju-88's. Beginning with 22 May 1941, the phrase "growing scarcity of bomber crews" occurs with ever greater frequency. (Der Ob.d.L., Generalquartiermeister 10-Tagemeldungen (Office of the Commander in Chief, Luftwaffe, Quartermaster General 10-Day Reports), Karlsruhe Document Collection.)

he held. If this superiority should be placed in doubt, as it was--
quantitatively and qualitatively--by British air armament activity,
then Germany's situation might soon experience a change for the worse.

This is presumably the motivation behind Hitler's request to Goering of October 1938; it is incomprehensible that the latter did not
pass it on to his closest associates until 6 December.[18]

The branch chiefs entrusted with the execution of Hitler's order
found it totally infeasible in view of the available aircraft factories,
schools, raw materials, and funds. As a compromise, the Chief of the
Organization Staff, Colonel Kammhuber,* worked out a modified program
of development. Even Kammhuber's program would have been difficult
enough to achieve, but it did guarantee a tremendous increase in Luftwaffe strength.

But Kammhuber's program was doomed to disapproval. Colonel Jeschonnek, at that time Chief of the Luftwaffe Operations Staff, insisted that
Hitler's original plan be followed to the letter. Jeschonnek managed
to convince both the State Secretary and Goering of the rightness of
his views and shortly thereafter, on 1 February 1939, was promoted to
Chief of the General Staff. Goering's approval, to be sure, was qualified; he stated that "everything possible" must be done to realize
Hitler's plan. In the last analysis, however, "everything possible"
turned out to be nothing at all. It was simply a comforting phrase,
which one could afterwards ignore.

In reality, the action taken resulted in no more than an accelera-
tion in the build-up of units recently activated. In other words, the
force already in being was brought more rapidly up to full strength;
the vitally necessary potential force (dependent upon more aircraft
works and an intensified training program) was not affected.

The excuse, that the beginning of the war (September 1939) made
all further preparatory activity impossible, is invalid. It is true
that neither new aircraft nor trained crews were available in the
sense of Hitler's demands. Even so, a program of expansion was feasible in many areas. If those in charge had been able to foresee the
developments of late 1940, one thing is certain; the General Staff
would have accustomed itself to thinking in terms of overall events
and large-scale requirements in the fields of aircraft production and
personnel training. In reality, however, Germany's leaders had gotten

_____

*Editor's Note: Later to become the first post World War II chief
of the German Air Force.

24

into the habit of tolerating apathy, improvisation, and stop-gap planning in both the air armament and pilot training programs, and this at a time when England was making an all-out effort in air armament, Russia was building up a tremendous air force, and America was beginning to develop its gigantic potential strength to a scope hitherto unimagined.

Nowhere do we find evidence of the Luftwaffe General Staff's having made a reasonable attempt to meet Hitler's demand for a fivefold increase in Luftwaffe strength. It was not until State Secretary Milch's intervention in 1942 and thereafter that the German air armament industry was finally roused from its unfortunate apathy. But the results of this intervention did not make themselves felt until 1943 and 1944, and by then it was already much too late. The training program, in spite of Milch's efforts, lagged far behind the requirements made upon it.

In its defense, though, we must admit that it had a number of very serious setbacks to overcome. These began with the raid on the training schools by the air fleet commanders. The second blow came when the Chief of Training was ordered to release his Ju-52's and his instructional crews for the setting up of special duty bomber groups* for employment in the airlanding operations in Norway and Holland and later--during the Balkan campaign--for the conquest of Crete.

No attempt was made to replace the losses thus incurred;[19] it was not until months later that the requisitioned aircraft, i.e. those which had escaped destruction, were returned to the Chief of Training. As regards the crews--consisting of carefully selected and carefully trained instructional personnel--it was an entirely different story. The best men among them obviously felt themselves far more attracted by service at the front than by training duty far behind the front lines, and pulled all the wires at their disposal to keep from returning to the schools. This source of loss, together with the death suffered by a great many instructors during their employment in air transport duty, represented a depletion in instructional personnel from which the office of the Chief of Training simply could not recover.

An attempt was made by Lt Colonel Deichmann--then Chief of Staff for the Chief of Training--to substitute the twin-engine Ju-86, which was not needed by any other Luftwaffe branch and for which the aircraft industry still had component parts for 1,000 aircraft, for the Ju-52's requisitioned during the air fleet raids on the training

---

*See below, page 33, which explains what actually happened to these units.

25

installations. Although Milch gave his approval to this plan, it was disapproved by Goering. Deichmann redoubled his efforts in this direction after the Norwegian campaign and defended his views during a conference with Goering. According to Deichmann[20] the Ju-86

> . . .could have been equipped with dual controls
> and a second instrument panel with relative ease
> and rapidity. Its crude-oil engine could have been
> replaced by a gasoline engine, and its excellent
> flight characteristics would have made it an ideal
> training machine. . . A further advantage was that
> the raw materials and parts needed to manufacture
> the Ju-86 were still readily available to industry
> in considerable supply, since the model had been
> dropped from the armament program without advance
> warning. A relatively small aircraft factory would
> have been quite capable of assembling the few air-
> craft needed for training purposes.

Deichmann continues: "My contention that the need for air transport services at the front would soon reach tremendous proportions was simply brushed aside. Feldmarschall Goering decided against my plan."

Deichmann's plan would have freed the Ju-52's for the air transport forces, and the training program could have proceeded without any uncertainty as to the availability of its most important training aircraft.

With disapproval of the Deichmann plan, an old evil (peacetime neglect of air transport) became apparent, and its consequences grew all the more painful as the demands for air transport services increased. It all began with the activation of a number of special duty bomber groups (in effect, air transport groups) in December 1941, when a major crisis on the Soviet front made it imperative that reinforcements be flown to the seriously threatened Army Group Center.

The second setback in the training program was not so justifiable as the first had been. When the decision was taken to initiate air supply services to certain isolated Army elements in Russia (a small group at Kholm and a larger unit--and for a period of more than several months--at Demyansk), it was the Chief of Training who was ordered to help out with newly activated units, some of them already equipped with He-111 bombers.

The air transport missions, which continued without hope of respite on the Russian front and were also beginning to be necessary in other theaters of war (Africa, the Channel ports), reached a peak with the air supply operations at Stalingrad, during which no fewer than 500 aircraft were lost.*

A further setback in the training program, already seriously weakened by continued requisitioning of its aircraft and instructional crews, was the gasoline situation. Ever since the middle of 1941, the training program had been treated like a step-child by the powers responsible for allocating gasoline, and in 1942 the allocation to the Chief of Training was restricted so tightly that only certain categories of personnel (and these only in limited number) could be trained. Every effort was made to conserve the dwindling gasoline stores, all the way down the line. In 1942 General von Seidel, the Quartermaster General, urged Jeschonnek to permit a more generous allocation of gasoline for training purposes. The General Staff Chief's reply was disheartening: "First we've got to beat Russia, then we can start training."[21] This incredible lack of understanding for the necessity of a training program as an integral part of the business of waging war can be explained only by the almost pathological blindness of an otherwise intelligent man, clinging to the forlorn hope that Russia could be conquered in a short war; and this in spite of Germany's experiences in the Soviet theater of operations.

The Chief of Training, whose prospects of functioning effectively were thus curtailed at every step, produced only a small number of trained fighter and bomber crews in the fall of 1942.[22] This was the year in which the training program all but ceased to exist as an effective entity.

In 1943, in order to keep up with the increase in aircraft production, the training program had no choice but to intensify its efforts and, by such measures as doubling up on training lessons, the lack of training aircraft and gasoline were compensated for to a certain degree. During 1944, however, when fighter aircraft production reached an unprecedented high, the training program--measured in terms of the effectiveness of the fighter crews trained--was hopelessly behind.

These, then, were the difficulties faced by the training program at a time when developments at the front--especially as regarded the need for fighter aircraft and crews--and in home air defense--becoming

----

*To be sure, this includes the losses suffered by the bomber units as well. See below, page 104.

more critical day by day--were giving the Luftwaffe no time to recuperate its strength in the unequal battle against superior numbers and superior quality. What good did it do to point out that there were finally ten fighter training schools,* all producing crew after crew in the shortened, hectic, and often interrupted training periods made necessary by existent conditions? The pilots' and crews' lack of familiarity with their aircraft⁺ and with the vagaries of weather caused a high incidence of loss and damage through crashes and crash landings. In addition, the enemy inflicted heavy losses by attacking with numerical superiority and superior machines. This is no wonder in view of the fact that the average German fighter pilot enjoyed a training period of 160 flying hours, completed in aircraft which sometimes bore very little resemblance to the fighters which he would later be required to fly. The British fighter pilot, on the other hand, was given 360 flying hours of training, and his American conterpart over 400, both in the most up-to-date fighter aircraft.[23]

Feldmarschall Milch may have exaggerated somewhat when he stated: "The Luftwaffe training program, and with it the Luftwaffe itself, was throttled to death by the gasoline shortage."[24] So much is undeniably true, however; the turning point in the air war was certainly due in great part to Germany's neglect of the training program and to the constant raids made upon its resources.

B. The Overestimation of Dive Bombing

Prior to the outbreak of the war, Germany had no really adequate bombsight[25] at her disposal. The Goerz-Visier 219 was effective "only in closely-limited areas and after a good deal of practice,"[26] and the optical sights, Lotfe 7 and 7D, were available in only a few experimental aircraft. The latter had not yet been incorporated into the training program.

Not even the best bomber crews from the Training Wing, using the Goerz-Visier 219, were able to achieve satisfactory results in area

---

*It may be pertinent to ask why it was suddenly possible to establish so many flight schools in the German Reich during 1944, at a time when the Reich was seriously weakened by enemy air attack on the German homeland and by the disheartening defeats at the front. Could these same schools not have been set up in Germany during 1939, 1940, or 1941?

⁺Due to the fact that the training program did not have a sufficient number of the newer fighter models at its disposal.

bombardment. The bomb-carrying capacity of the German bombers was relatively low (one 550-lb. bomb for the Do-17; four 550-lb. bombs for the He-111).* Thus, even though a bomber unit might drop an impressive number of bombs in an area bombardment action, the individual performance of each aircraft was comparatively slight. In dive-bomber attacks, on the other hand, the results achieved by the Training Wing during its practice runs were impressive indeed.†

Consequently, the technique of attack by individual dive bombers seemed to be an extremely appropriate method, worthy of further development. The Luftwaffe had at its disposal well-trained, enthusiastic crews, accustomed to the carefully tested Ju-87,‡ and it is quite understandable that Luftwaffe leaders had great confidence in the immediate effectiveness of this weapon in case of war.

Pin-point bombing, with the dive bomber releasing its load directly over the target, seemed to promise a high degree of bombing precision and appeared to be exactly the right method for Germany's situation. For Germany, in the words of a member of the Luftwaffe command hierarchy, "was so limited with regard to raw materials and gasoline that her production capacity and, in turn, her war potential, simply did not permit the construction of sufficient numbers of heavy bomber fleets. She had no choice but to limit herself to medium and light bombers with the highest possible degree of hitting accuracy."[27] Eberhard Spetzler, from whom the foregoing was quoted, goes on to say that a preference for precision bombing "was quite natural to Germany, since it was in keeping with the continental concept of the conduct of war," and as this concept applied to air warfare, it called for maximum precision in hitting a militarily significant target--normally a relatively small area--with a minimum of danger to the surrounding countryside. Spetzler continues, "Hitler, who repeatedly spoke up for the abolition of the

---

*Editor's Note: The Dornier-17 and the Heinkel-111 were both twin-engine bombers.

†In 1938, "on the occasion of a demonstration before Hitler by the Bomber Group Greifswald/Barth, the dive-bombers made a very impressive showing over practice targets at Zingst. Even then, there was a long discussion afterwards among the younger Luftwaffe officers as to whether it might not be possible to develop long-range dive-bombers." (Reported to the author on 18 April 1956 by Major a. D. Helmuth Pohle.)

‡Editor's Note: The Ju(Junkers)-87 was the famous "Stuka" dive-bomber, a two-place aircraft with a low, inverted, gull wing.

bombardment war, was just as eager as Goering to spare the civilian population of both sides the horrors of air warfare insofar as possible. . . ."

In view of all this, it is perfectly understandable that the youthful Luftwaffe General Staff Chief, Jeschonnek, and the colleagues whom he had recruited from the Training Wing (particularly Captain Helmuth Pohle) were just as enthusiastic about this bombardment technique as the crews of the dive-bomber groups themselves. Further, it is understandable that a daring pilot like Udet was much more deeply impressed by the tactical offensive possible with dive bombers than by the mere releasing of bombs by a fleet of heavy bombers flying in a horizontal line at high altitude. In fact Udet—a devotee of broad humor—even invented special whistles (the so-called Trumpets of Jericho) to attach to the bombs carried by the Ju-87's, their purpose being to put the fear of God and the Last Judgment into the victims of the attack.

The enthusiastic champions of the dive-bomber technique were blind to its disadvantages. Chief among these was the dive bomber's vulnerability at the moment in which the pilot pulled out of his dive. And this became more and more dangerous as the defenders became accustomed to dive-bomber attack and persisted in their antiaircraft artillery fire. Moreover, during the moment when the pilot was pulling out of his dive, his machine was completely defenseless against attacking fighter aircraft.

"The dive," writes General Krauss, "presents an extremely difficult problem in aeronautics. Only the best pilots are capable of carrying it through so that they really hit their targets, and that only after long practice. . . ."[28] General Krauss continues: "In the concentrated demand for dive bombers, one fact was completely overlooked: the hitting accuracy achieved during a dive depends necessarily upon the bomb-release altitude and upon the pilot's knowledge of wind conditions at that altitude. The reflector sight was effective only at relatively low release altitudes. The BZA-2* was still in the developmental stage. . . In addition, the Luftwaffe did not get around to setting up a bombardment school (in Anklam) until the war began in 1939."[†]

The Luftwaffe General Staff had rejected the concept of area bombardment and had decided to concentrate on pinpoint bombardment.

---

*Bombsight, type 2.

†Uncomprehending astonishment is the only possible reaction to this fact!

30

In the tactical requirements summary issued by the General Staff in the spring of 1938, the following appears: "The emphasis in offensive bombardment has clearly shifted from area to pinpoint bombardment. For this reason, the development of a bombsight suitable for use in dive-bomber aircraft is more important than the development of any other aiming device."[29]

The step from pinpoint bombing by a unit to pinpoint bombing by a single aircraft was a short one and, as a matter of fact, quite a logical one. For example, if the target was that particular part of a factory which was indispensible to the operation of the whole,[30] then a single, highly-qualified crew was all that was needed. In addition to being effective, the method also gave promise of being the most economical.

During the Battle of Britain, when the early bomber fleet raids had resulted in heavy losses without achieving any decisive results, Jeschonnek--the foremost champion of the pinpoint bombardment technique--picked out particularly efficient crews to carry out individual raids. As a result, British air defense elements (fighters and anti-aircraft artillery) were able to concentrate all their efforts on these individual aircraft, which were, of course, picked up by British radar in plenty of time. The losses thus incurred--irrevocable losses, since the very least that could happen was that the crews were taken prisoner-- involved the elite among Luftwaffe flying personnel, and even at that time they were difficult, if not impossible, to replace.

Without really intending to and perhaps without even realizing it, the General Staff Chief and his staff--in their shift from the concept of area bombing to that of pinpoint bombardment and individual attack-- got farther and farther away from the idea of strategic air warfare, to which they still adhered in theory. But strategic air warfare, with its goal of paralyzing or destroying the enemy's sources of military strength, had very little in common with these individual attacks (pin-pricks!), which were usually ineffective and never decisive and could almost always be repulsed if the enemy marshalled his antiaircraft defenses cleverly. Success in strategic air warfare, on the other hand, depends upon the employment of concentrated forces of ever-increasing strength in an effort to destroy all the enemy's military potential, and such employment must be repeated again and again until a decision is reached.

The consequences of the Luftwaffe's preference for pinpoint bombardment by dive-bomber will be discussed in greater detail later on.

31

C. Neglect of the Air Transport Forces

During the early developmental days of the new Luftwaffe, Hitler
and Luftwaffe leaders were confronted by the problem of air transport,
and their handling of it was a foreshadowing of events to come.

On 26 July 1936, while Hitler was in Bayreuth for the Wagner Festi-
val, he was visited by representatives of General Franco, who was then
engaged in the struggle against the popular front government in Madrid.
Franco requested that Hitler place at his disposal a number of Luftwaffe
transport aircraft to bring the Spanish Foreign Legion, as well as
Moroccan troops, from Tetuan to Seville. Hitler immediately approved
the loan of twenty Ju-52's and their crews. The first one (under the
command of Lufthansa Captain Jenke) took off from Berlin-Tempelhof the
very next day, 27 July 1936, and the other nineteen followed shortly.

The tremendous significance of this undertaking was soon apparent.
Each machine was capable of transporting 22-30 men with their equipment
and, if necessary, could make the Tetuan-Seville trip four times a day.
There is no question but that the air transport service furnished by
Germany, coming as it did during the first, most decisive days of the
Franco uprising, was one of the main factors enabling the Spanish
Dictator to consolidate his position so quickly, i.e. to secure a firm
base of operations for his offensive against the government.[31]

In the face of this object lesson, carried out by German transport
aircraft with an escort of German fighters before the eyes of an interested and observant Europe, it seems incredible that the German General
Staff--and particularly the Luftwaffe General Staff--should not have
been immediately won over to the importance of air transport. Franco's
action in transporting military forces over long distances by air gave
ample evidence of the feasibility, in the event of a future war, of
sudden attacks in unexpected areas. Even during World War I the importance of troop transport had been clearly demonstrated when General
Maunoury's army was transported by the Paris taxis to the right flank
of the German offensive wing (the German First Army under Generaloberst
von Kluck).

Even so, Franco's air transport of the Moroccan troops failed to
move the Luftwaffe to create an independent air transport force, with
its own corps of specially trained officers. Nor did it give rise to
a call for increased production of the Ju-52, which was the ideal
transport aircraft. On the contrary, in 1937, when production was curtailed because of a reduction in steel and aluminum allocations, the
Ju-52's were the hardest hit of all aircraft types.

This was particularly unfortunate because, as has already been mentioned, the Ju-52 played an extremely important role in the Luftwaffe training program and was never replaced by an aircraft model created exclusively for training purposes. As a result, the training program was pretty well tied to the Ju-52, and the Ju-52, unfortunately, was very attractive for all sorts of other uses. Until 1943, all the requests for Ju-52's were filled at the cost of the Chief of Training.

New production of Ju-52's never reached the point at which the requirements of both, i.e. of the training program and the air transport forces, could be filled adequately. Ever since the setbacks suffered by Germany on the Russian front (and especially after Stalingrad, which frustrated completely all subsequent attempts to stabilize the front), there had been more and more requests for air transport forces--for troop transports, air supply missions, and airlift actions-- and all of these took their toll of the overall strength of the Luftwaffe. The air transport forces, already overburdened with their missions in Tunisia,* were unable to get back up to full strength. They were swept on into the catastrophe to its very end (the air supply action at Breslau), and by the close of the war they were totally depleted. Although they were finally (1 October 1944) consolidated under the command of an Air Transport Chief directly subordinate to the Commander in Chief, Luftwaffe, the air transport forces still had no channel through which they could argue for refusal of undertakings which were obviously hopeless from the beginning, i.e. in which the end result was not sufficiently important to justify the sacrifices involved. They had no choice but to obey, to sanction the commitment of their very last forces, until the end came.

In view of this unfortunate--indeed, fatal--course of development, it seems utterly grotesque that from 1 October 1941 until April 1942, the Chief of the Instrument Flight Schools, Office of the Chief of Training, was expected to double as Air Transport Chief. The Chief of Training was understandably reluctant to relinquish his influence over the Air Transport Chief (otherwise he probably would never have gotten his training aircraft back); the latter had his own air transport staff and was stationed with it at Smolensk. At the same time, as Chief of the Instrument Flight Schools, he headed a training staff (to which, of course, he could devote no time whatsoever) located in the office of the Chief of Training. This is a particularly good example of the violation of the traditional proverb which warns against attempting to serve two masters at the same time.

When Germany finally instituted a training program for air

---

*After 15 May 1943 the air transport forces were concentrated in the XIVth Air Force.

transport personnel, it was not due to the object lesson presented by Franco or even to Germany's own belated recognition of the necessity for some means of rapid troop transport; it was due exclusively to the Russian experiments with paratrooper forces, which were so disquieting that Germany even set up paratrooper units of her own.

It was at about this time that the German bomber wings were converted from the Ju-52, never ideal as a bomber, to the He-111, which had recently gone into series production. The only unit to retain its Ju-52's was the IVth Group of the Bomber Wing Hindenburg. The IVth Group was placed at the disposal of the paratroop battalion then being activated and was intended to serve as a nucleus for the formation of additional units of the same type. In October 1937, the IVth Group was rechristened the 1st Special Duty Bomber Group and was later assigned to the 7th (Paratroop) Division. On 1 August 1938, the Group was divided and each half-group then brought up to full strength, and during the summer of 1939 (just before the beginning of the war), the 1st Special Duty Bomber Group was expanded into a "fully-recognized, active air transport unit," the counterpart of the paratroop regiment. At about this time, preparations were begun for the activation of a second paratroop regiment; a corresponding second special duty bomber group, however, was not activated.

The status of the air transport forces was rather an inferior one; they did not even have an air fleet of their own to take its place among the other four air fleets already in existence, but were merely a wing subordinate to the 7th Air Division.

It is obvious that the air transport forces, by virtue of their ridiculously subaltern position on the organizational scale, were deprived of a good many advantages which they might otherwise have enjoyed. The establishment of an independent air transport fleet would have necessitated the appointment of an air fleet commander in chief with a staff made up of General Staff officers. The problems of day by day administration would have necessitated greater clarity in organizational thinking. Automatically, the problems faced by the air transport forces would have been taken into consideration and solutions worked out during the periodic war games. Experienced and high-ranking specialists, whose opinions could not be brushed aside without further ado, would have been on hand to consider the questions arising in connection with the first large-scale air supply operations in the Russian theater of war. The existence of such a staff would have provided a certain measure of protection against the uneconomical employment of air transport aircraft in senseless air supply actions such as the ones at Kholm and Demyansk, not to mention the completely hopeless ones, of which Stalingrad is the best example.

The actual situation was quite different. Unfortunately, even the highest-ranking air transport officers were nothing more than recipients of orders from above; because of their comparatively lower rank, they were not even consulted as to the feasibility of the large-scale transport operations ordered by the Luftwaffe top-level command. Let us consider the example of Stalingrad. If there had been an air transport fleet, is it likely that Hitler would have consulted only the Commander in Chief of the Luftwaffe and the latter's General Staff Chief? Or, if Hitler had not turned to the transport fleet commander on his own initiative, is it not reasonable to suppose that Generaloberst Zeitzler, for example, who was dead set against air supply operations on behalf of the encircled Sixth Army, would have persuaded Hitler at least to listen to his opinion?

In a study by Generalmajor a. D. Fritz Morzik, former Air Transport Chief, the author states that before launching an airlift, ". . . every possible effort must have been made to obviate the necessity for one."[32] General Morzik, who wrote this study in close collaboration with the officers who played important roles in air transport activity, continues: "During World War I air transport had no opportunity to make a place for itself. . . ."[33] It was not until the period between the two wars that this opportunity presented itself in the form of the tremendous increase in commercial flying. It is incomprehensible that military leaders paid so little attention to the military possibilities of this new mode of transport.

In any case, it was not until World War II that the versatility of an aircraft type designed for transport purposes and its consequent potential value to a modern military force could be demonstrated. The employment of transport aircraft was not the result of a planned period of systematic development; there was no body of past experience on which to build, and no guidelines had been developed regarding the potentialities and limitations of transport aircraft. What little systematic planning that had been done viewed the commitment of transport aircraft as a means of transport for parachute and air landing forces. It must be emphasized at this point, as it has been elsewhere, that Germany's failure to recognize the potentialities inherent in the transport aircraft was a basic and serious mistake. And one cannot resist the temptation to add that this mistake not only led to the decimation of the air transport forces, but was also responsible in good part for the loss of the war.

III - <u>Errors in the Field of Operational and Technical Requirements</u>.

A. <u>Adherence to the Dive-Bomber Concept and its Effects on Germany's Bomber Arm</u>.

We have already seen how Jeschonnek and the General Staff had pledged themselves to the concept of the dive bomber and its employment against pinpoint targets and had rejected the concept of area bombardment. As has been pointed out, this development was chiefly responsible for the inadequacy of the German bombsights.

As a matter of fact, under the limitations already described, the dive-bomber idea was a reasonable one. Yet its development provides a perfect example of the way in which a perfectly good idea can be so exaggerated that it leads to the downfall of an entire service branch.

The idea was originally Udet's. In 1933, with Milch's approval, he brought back to Germany two American dive bombers (Curtiss Hawks). It was due to Udet's foresight that the dive-bomber principle was modified for use with a single-engine machine. The German Ju-87, ready for production by 1936, was a dependable instrument and its stability and robust construction were points in its favor. It was relatively slow, however, and for this reason had to be withdrawn from commitment against the British as early as 1940. On the Eastern front, on the other hand, it remained in action until the autumn of 1943 and rendered valuable assistance to the hard-pressed German ground forces in close-support operations.

All this was still far in the future in 1938, however, when the Luftwaffe General Staff, enthusiastic over the target accuracy demonstrated by the Ju-87 Group at Greifswald-Barth, ordered Junkers engineers to modify the twin-engine bomber they were working on (a longer-range, fast bomber) to include diving performance. As a result of this new requirement, which necessitated a more stable fuselage construction as well as the installation of diving brakes and a number of other extras, the flying weight of the Ju-88, originally planned for six tons, increased to twelve or thirteen tons. The good old Ju-87 weighed only about one-third as much, 4.2 tons.[34] It was obvious that a dive with the Ju-88 was going to be a far more difficult undertaking than it was with the Ju-87. Even an average crew could manage a creditable dive with the latter. An additional warning occurred when Captain Rudolf Freiherr (Baron) von Moreau, an experienced pilot who had seen service with the Condor Legion in Spain, crashed to his death in a Ju-88 at Rechlin. At this juncture, Jeschonnek ordered Captain Hellmuth Pohle to set up a testing group and to fly the machine himself. This gave an experienced pilot, who was himself an avid champion of the dive-bomber idea, a chance to try out the Ju-88. After a two weeks' trial, Pohle reported to the General Staff his confidence that even an average crew could learn to negotiate an 80°-dive with the Ju-88 with sufficient training and practice; unfortunately, Pohle's confidence was never justified. In action over Malta and against naval targets, the Ju-88 did attain the performance promised for it. On the whole, though, the tendency "in the field" was towards "far too shallow dives . . . some of those measured were no more than 30°."[35] At this angle, of course, rocket bombs were completely ineffective against armored targets, and the painstaking work devoted to their development was in vain.[36]

If the General Staff had not ordered these modifications in the spring of 1938, the Ju-88 would no doubt have been ready for use far earlier and the Luftwaffe would have had a fast, long-range bomber at its disposal.

General a. D. Marquardt, (Engineer Corps), who is firmly convinced that it was the dive-bomber concept which brought ultimate ruin to the German Luftwaffe, speaks of the two Curtiss Hawks which Udet brought back from the United States as ". . .Trojan horses within the walls of traditional aircraft design." Goering, "as an old fighter pilot, was understandably enthusiastic about the idea of a dive bomber." Marquardt continues, "the bomber pilots from World War I, no longer active pilots but holding important positions in the Luftwaffe command hierarchy, didn't dare to object to the dive-bomber concept for fear of being thought 'old-fashioned.'"[37] According to Marquardt, the General Staff simply did not understand the principle pointed out by the technical experts, namely that "in aircraft development, those qualities ought to be emphasized which serve to make the aircraft different from all other military vehicles, in other words those attributes which enable it to overcome the obstacles of distance and time and so to achieve its maximum effect." "In the dive bomber," Marquardt points out, "it is precisely these attributes which are sacrificed, because it must utilize brakes to reduce its attacking speed and because, in order to be able to release its bombs from a relatively low altitude in the interests of maximum accuracy, it is forced to descend into the effective range of enemy antiaircraft artillery fire."*

---

*Marquardt is not quite so rigorous in applying these same objections to the Ju-87: "The relatively light-weight Ju-87, to be sure, was another matter. Its construction was well thought-out; it was simple in both maintenance and employment, and as long as the enemy antiaircraft defenses were comparatively weak, it rendered excellent service in combined commitment with the ground forces. The only question was whether or not we really needed a special aircraft type for this purpose." (Marquardt study.)

37

Yet Luftwaffe leaders clung to the dive-bomber concept with a stubbornness explainable only on the basis of sheer blindness. Horizontal bombardment was completely out of the picture as far as they were concerned.

Once an idea has taken exclusive possession of men's minds, fate itself is powerless to drive it out again; the mind becomes inaccessible to the lessons of experience, no matter how impressive they may be. The dive bomber might almost be termed the idol of the Luftwaffe General Staff. Before experience with the Ju-88 had begun to reveal its unsuitability as a dive bomber, the General Staff had already given instructions to incorporate diving ability into the long-range bomber He-177 (which had a flying weight of thirty-two tons), then in process of development at the Heinkel works. Because of this new requirement, Heinkel engineers decided to make use of a design already developed in connection with a twin-engine model, in which two engines were combined tandem-fashion to drive one propeller, instead of utilizing the more stable design of four independently functioning engines.

In practice, however, the use of two engines with a single propeller proved to be a source of danger since the engines repeatedly caught fire. As a result, crashes involving the loss of both aircraft and crew were common.* Finally--but far too late in view of the overall military situation--the decision was made to return to the original four-engine design for the He-177. In this connection, Goering, when it was explained to him on 13 September 1942 that tandem engines were a prerequisite if adequate diving performance was to be achieved, told Heinkel in no uncertain terms: "What an asinine idea, to demand diving ability of a four-engine aircraft! If they had consulted me, I could have told them right away that that was nonsense. A four-engine bomber doesn't have to be able to dive. I'll be satisfied when we have a twin-engine model that far along. So far we've managed perfect dives only with a single-engine machine, the old Iolanthe /Ju-87/ . . . It's perfectly idiotic to expect a four-engine bomber to dive. If I had known, I would have gone right to the top. . . ." To Heinkel's rejoinder, "A dive with a machine weighing thirty tons is a colossal undertaking; it's never yet been done in the history of the world . . .", Goering replied: "And it isn't going to be done in the history of the world - at least not under my supervision . . . I'm grateful when a four-engine bomber can even fly at a 30° angle - it would be sheer madness to try to dive in one!" On 22 February 1943, Goering once more spoke out against the tandem engines.[38] But in order not to lose all the work which had gone into

---

*Marquardt speaks of fifty crews lost during the testing period alone; five more were lost during the air supply operations at Stalingrad. (Marquardt study.)

their development thus far, it was decided to keep on experimenting with them. By the time the General Staff finally changed its mind and made the reluctant decision to go back to the original design of four independently functioning engines, it was too late to do very much good. An experimental model was ready for testing by 1944, but it never reached the stage of mass production. In the report of a fighter staff conference which took place on 3 July 1944, the following appears:[39]

> . . . In a conference lasting nearly five hours with the Reichsmarschall on Saturday, we were told that the old He-177 will be pulled out of production as soon as those few machines now being finished are out of the way, and that the entire labor force concerned will be freed for our use in other programs. Moreover, it was decided not to start production on the new He-177, not even in limited numbers. This means that the entire working plant--labor force, equipment, and everything else--is at our disposal.

A little more than ten months later, Germany's ruin was complete. It is certain that the tragedy of the He-177 was one of the factors which had contributed to her downfall.

The He-177 was not the only aircraft model involved, however. According to Heinkel,[40] Udet once told him that the He-111 would be Germany's last horizontal-flight bomber. When it was decided to construct a more modern engine for the Me-110 long-range fighter* in order to fit it for commitment as a fast bomber (the idea was that it would ultimately replace the Ju-87), the General Staff was on hand once again with its demands that diving performance be included in the requirements. It was partly this requirement which rendered the new model, the Me-210,⧸ perfectly useless.⧸ Because industry had made extremely

---

*Editor's Note: A low-wing, twin-engine fighter manufactured by Messerschmitt.

⧸Editor's Note: A twin-engine, long-range fighter-bomber; also made by Messerschmitt.

⧸Here it must be emphasized that the General Staff requirement was only partly responsible for the Me-210 fiasco. Messerschmitt's lack of caution in making assurances and promises to high-level agencies; his indifference to further developments once the original design had been approved; the almost constant changes in the requirements set up by the General Staff (influenced by the fatal concept of an "all-purpose"

time-consuming and expensive preparations for the production of the Me-210, the waste in labor hours and working area and the losses involved in scrapped materials were particularly conspicuous.[41]

General Marquardt estimates that approximately 10,000 aircraft engines of the DB-601 type went to waste during the period 1941-1943 (the very years during which the basis for subsequent military events was being established), partly, of course, as a result of circumstances beyond anyone's control, but also because of the fact that the General Staff remained adamant in its requirement of diving performance for the He-177 and the Me-210. As Marquardt points out, if this requirement (which was beyond fulfillment in any case*) had not existed, Germany could have sent 10,000 more fighter aircraft to the front.

Marquardt expresses himself as follows: "The military situation would have been entirely different if we had had 10,000 more fighter aircraft--this would have been twice as many as we really had--at the front at that time.⌐ As it was, all our materiel was tied up in useless equipment; this is the real reason for the defeat of the German Luftwaffe."

Marquardt's words should perhaps be modified in one or two minor respects, but we cannot deny that the decision of the two most influential Luftwaffe agencies, the Technical Office and the General Staff, to concentrate exclusively on the dive bomber was one of the factors, originating before World War II even began, which were to lead to a turning point in the air war.

B. The Four-Engine Bomber.

Ever since 1933, the German air armament program had concerned itself with the construction of a four-engine bomber.

---

aircraft); the carelessness of the Technical Office in permitting mass production planning to proceed for a model which had not yet been adequately tested; the interference of a number of influential flying personalities; all of these factors contributed to the end result. As can be seen, the problem is not so simple as Marquardt--in search of support for his thesis--would have us think. Nevertheless, it cannot be denied that the "dive-bomber" requirement did play a part in the catastrophe of the Me-210.

*According to Marquardt, the He-177 was only sporadically able to achieve a diving angle of 25-30°. (Marquardt study.)

⌐When he used the phrase "at that time," Marquardt refers to the "decisive" years 1942 and 1943. (Marquardt study.)

Colonel Wimmer, then Chief of the Technical Office, was successful in his efforts to persuade Colonel Wever--at that time Chief of the Miscellaneous Branch of the Reichs Air Ministry--of the need to develop a heavy bomber. Wimmer pointed out that it would take at least three years' work before even a small number of bombers could be ready for testing in the units. Failure to take the necessary steps right away would result in valuable time irrevocably lost once the problem became acute.[42]

Wever was convinced. He began to count on the heavy (four-engine) bomber as a decisive weapon in the event of serious hostilities. Within the Reichs Air Ministry the machine was christened "Uralbomber" (Ural bomber), a clear indication of the range expected of it.[43]

By 1936 the two firms entrusted with its development had two designs ready, the Ju-89 and the Do-19. According to General Deichmann, who at that time was Chief of Branch 1 (Operations) of the Luftwaffe General Staff, both models were perfectly adequate as a basis for further development, although both were equipped with relatively weak engines.[44] Feldmarschall Milch concurs in General Deichmann's evaluation.[45] At this point, however, instead of going ahead with the developmental work (and designing more powerful engines), Goering ordered a halt on all work concerned with the four-engine bomber. And this despite the fact that both models appeared in the Technical Office (Development Branch) priority list (dated 26 April 1937 and reflecting the status of 15 March 1937) as "SV" (Models ready for testing). According to the testimony given by Feldmarschall Milch at Nuremberg,[46] General Kesselring (then General Staff Chief) had requested, and obtained a halt from Goering on 29 April. Deichmann, on the other hand, emphasizes Milch's role in this decision. Udet, who became General Wimmer's successor as Chief of the Technical Office on 10 June 1936, must also be ranked with the enemies of the four-engine bomber, as must his branch chief, von Massenbach, and a number of other Technical Office engineers.

Suffice it to say that the four-engine bomber was definitely dropped in the spring of 1937. As a result, Germany never developed this particular weapon, perhaps the most important instrument in strategic air warfare.

To be sure, soon after this unfortunate decision had been made (even earlier, in the fall of 1936, according to Generalingenieur a. D. Huebner, who at that time was a staff assistant for development in the Technical Office),[47] the General Staff began to call for a long-range bomber, its range to be approximately double that of the two four-engine models already designed. Most unfortunately the idea of making this long-range bomber a twin-engine machine soon gained a foothold, whereupon Heinkel (who, in addition to Junkers, had been asked to work on development) suggested that his test model, the He-119, might be used as a starting point. Careful study of the He-119 resulted in the decision to solve the problem of four engines by utilizing two sets of engines in tandem arrangement. We have already discussed the relationship of this system to the diving-performance requirement set up by the General Staff. It was chiefly due to the use of this system that the He-117 was never developed into a satisfactory model.

In part, of course, the catastrophe was also due to a lack of consistency in overall aims. From the very beginning, political aspects were permitted to interfere in the development of the long-range bomber. For it was largely political considerations which dictated the constant alternation between high and low developmental priority; one day work would be slowed down because the machine was not urgently needed, and the next day orders would be issued to go ahead on it as rapidly as possible. Conditions were hardly conducive to a well-founded, carefully thought-out course of development.

Prior to the beginning of the war, the prevailing mood was one of optimism. There would be no war with England because...well, simply because Germany did not want war with England. And if the British should adopt a hostile attitude towards Germany, there was always Hitler, whose genius would certainly manage to find a peaceful solution. Under these circumstances, Luftwaffe leaders did not consider the development of a long-range bomber to be particularly necessary or urgent, especially since they were confident that the range of the Ju-88 would enable it to cover not only the British Isles in their entirety but the coastal waters beyond as well. And at that time, of course, no one had any idea that a war with Russia was even remotely possible. The name "Ural bomber" was forgotten, and with it all the significance which Wever, in his astute evaluation of future events, attached to the long-range bomber for Germany.*

The He-177 was the victim of this optimistic attitude. Its development was not pushed hard enough before the war began. With the sobering shock of England's declaration of war, efforts were redoubled, only to subside again as the blitz attacks on the London area proved to be so successful. As war with Soviet Russia loomed imminent and finally became a reality, new and even more urgent efforts were made to push

------

*Even so, Hitler's program for a fivefold increase in Luftwaffe strength did envision the activation of long-range bomber units.

ahead on the He-177. Apart from all this uncertainty, however, there
still remained the problem--never fully appreciated--of the unfeasi-
bility of the tandem-engine design. Because of this, Germany failed
to make the shift to four independently functioning engines in time.
As we have seen, this failure in the armament sector--and the losses
attributable to it--was one of the deciding factors in the outcome of
the war.

Let us pause for a moment to consider the possibility so casually
renounced in 1937, of a genuine four-engine bomber at the disposal of
the German Air Force. Its significance in naval warfare (North Sea,
Polar Sea, Atlantic) could have been enormous, especially during the
early stages of the war; later on, the Allied convoys to Murmansk would
have been vulnerable for a far longer stretch of their route to a hail
of bombs from these powerful, high-altitude, heavily-armored bombers.
In the Battle of Britain, too, long-range bombers could have created
an entirely different situation, due to the qualities pointed out above
and to their ability to appear anywhere over the British Isles. British
antiaircraft defenses, admirably developed for use against the German
medium bombers, would have been so thoroughly dissipated by long-range
bombers that defeat would have been inevitable. In the Russian campaign, with the tremendous distances inherent in its geographic scope,
long-range bombers would have been able to search out and destroy the
centers of Soviet military armament. Heavily armored as they were,
they would have been relatively invulnerable to Russian fighter aircraft; their flight altitude would have been sufficient to render antiaircraft artillery useless. There is one other aspect to be considered:
if Germany had had four-engine bomber units at her disposal, her Army
forces in Russia--no matter how enamoured of the concept of ground-air
operations--would never have thought of requesting close-support action
from the larger aircraft.

In closing, let us consider what effect the employment of four-
engine bombers would have had in the Mediterranean, against the Suez
Canal and other weak points in the British line of defense. Our thesis
can be amply illustrated by one example. Prior to the Allied landing
in North Africa, German leaders were fully aware of the fact that the
Gibraltar airfields were crowded with enemy aircraft; however, because
of the limited range of its bombers, the Luftwaffe was unable to launch
an attack, although this would have been tremendously successful and
would have made an Allied occupation of western North Africa extremely
hazardous. Such an attack would have presented no problem for four-
engine bombers. In addition, the enemy's transport fleet could have
been under continual attack.

43

But enough of these potentialities which never reached fulfillment.
The fact remains that the sins of omission and errors in judgment in
this particular field were one of the factors leading to the final
collapse. One more point lost to the German Reich in the field of
armament planning!

Chapter 2

FURTHER PROGRESS TOWARDS DEFEAT

I - Areas of Neglect and Error during the War

As far as wartime errors and wrong decisions on the part of Luftwaffe leaders are concerned, we are dealing with events which, although they occurred well before the actual turning point, had a significant influence on the history of the Luftwaffe. For these events, far more than those which occurred prior to the beginning of the war, were to play a vital role in subsequent military developments. The Luftwaffe, despite the tremendous successes it was to enjoy in the eyes of the world, already bore the seeds of defeat in the form of defects traceable to faulty prewar planning. And these defects, as we have seen, were by no means minor, incidental ones. The Luftwaffe, still new and untried, had been designed for blitzkrieg operations, and in three brilliant campaigns of this type was to prove its value as the backbone of the Wehrmacht. It must not be forgotten, however, that the Luftwaffe was far less capable than the Army of recovering from serious setbacks or heavy losses. The replacement of both materiel (aircraft and equipment) and personnel was far more difficult, for the production of aircraft and the training of crews were both time-consuming affairs. Everything depended upon timely preparation. Above all, it was vital that the development of new weapons be systematically planned and brought to fruition in order that they might be ready for employment at the front before those already in use were outmoded and inferior to those used by the enemy.

In the case of the Luftwaffe, the mistakes and instances of neglect which occurred during wartime and which were based, in part, on the Luftwaffe's prewar weaknesses, were to have far-reaching consequences.

A. The Lack of Economic Mobilization and the Relative Insignificance of Production during the Period 1939-1942

As early as 1935, specific instructions indicating the steps to be taken in case of war had been issued to the German air armament industry. Even during peacetime, this so-called mobilization plan was recognized as having "highest authority for over-all planning." While the peacetime production program was based on a single work shift of eight hours per day, the mobilization plan called for two shifts of eight to ten hours per day. Peacetime and wartime production programs had been carefully planned so that a smooth and rapid shift could be made to the latter

45

without the necessity of constructing and equipping additional work
space. The industry had been instructed ahead of time to install the
equipment necessary to meet the scope of production called for by the
mobilization plan, to see that construction projects outside the main
works were protected insofar as possible from the danger of bombardment, and to keep on hand sufficient raw materials to last for six
months. Each factory had a mobilization planning office staffed by
personnel trained by the Defense Inspectorates and found to be compe-
tent and reliable. This office was responsible for the preparation of
a mobilization calendar which was subject to periodic inspection by
Defense Inspectorate officials; these, in turn, were empowered to adjust
it in keeping with any changes made in the overall program. In this
way, difficulties and bottlenecks--to a certain extent at least--could
be foreseen and eliminated. During 1935 and 1936 the Technical Office
carried out test mobilization in a number of factories, and the experience thus gained was of great value.

Thus thoroughgoing planning, characterized by the careful attempt
to eliminate in advance any possible difficulties, was carried out to
prepare the German aircraft industry for an immediate increase in production as soon as the war should begin.

It was highly unfortunate, of course, that by the beginning of 1937
the available construction capacity allotted to the aircraft industry
had already been used up and, because of the shortage in iron (still
readily available, however, for a number of other projects), the build-
up of the air armament industry was forced to a stop. This was followed
by a "far-reaching curtailment of funds for the Armed Forces," which
naturally necessitated a curtailment in aircraft production. "If the
build-up could have proceeded systematically and without interruption,"
says Generalingenieur a. D. Walter Hertel, "there is no doubt but that
aircraft production capacity would have been much greater by the time
the war began."[1]

During the war itself, "the independence of the various Armed
Forces Branches and the lack of uniform guidance of the armament program" continued to be an unfavorable factor "as far as maximum exploita-
tion of the available work-force and construction capacity was concerned."[2] It was not until 1 May 1944 that the entire construction
program was placed under the supervision of Ministry Director Dorsch
of the Reichs Ministry of Armament and War Economy. This action came
too late. The mobilization of the economy, the plans for which had been
so carefully laid, never materialized. It is not within the purview

46

of this study to investigate the reasons for this failure;* its consequences are obvious from the positively pitiful production figures recorded during the early years of the war. Total aircraft production for the first four months was less than during the corresponding period of 1945, at a time when the Reich was nearing final collapse and, having lost large portions of her territory, was almost entirely defenseless in the face of enemy air attack. The increase in production during 1940

---

*The failure of economic mobilization seems to be a fact which is taken for granted; no attempt is made to explain the reasons behind it. Presumably it had something to do, at least in part, with Hitler's self-deception in regard to the will for peace of his enemies in the West. General der Artillerie a. D. Walter Warlimont, has the following to say in a letter to the author under date of 27 December 1957:

> In the face of the successful Polish campaign, Hitler refused to order mobilization in the full sense of the word; later on, partial mobilization was ordered, but the economy was specifically exempted. This business of the "gradual establishment of increased military preparedness," as it was called, in preparation for "special commitment of the Armed Forces" brought nothing but confusion, as I can testify from personal experience---the tragedy of which I shall never be able to forget. To put it briefly, none of the carefully thought-out measures designed to protect the armament industry by keeping its skilled workers on the job was put into effect. Not until it was no longer possible to ignore the fact that the West meant business was any attempt made to undo the damage. By then, of course, it was no longer a matter of putting a certain paragraph of the mobilization plan into effect, but of ordering back every single skilled worker from the front, provided of course, that he was still among the living.

The failure of economic mobilization and its effects on the Luftwaffe are problems worthy of more detailed investigation. Editor's Note: General Warlimont, referred to above, was deputy chief of the Armed Forces Operations Staff during the war, and considered, by his colleagues, to be a particularly gifted young officer. In Nuremberg, in 1948, General Warlimont was sentenced to life imprisonment as a war criminal. His sentence was later reduced and he has since been released on parole.

was slight, but even at that it was greater than the increase recorded for 1941, despite the fact that this was the year in which Germany dared to pit her strength against that of Soviet Russia. Furthermore, we find these same figures for years during which the Polish and French campaigns had already brought the raw materials and the production capacity of the West into the German camp, years in which the following factors existed and should have been exploited:

1. The German aircraft and aircraft engine factories were able to carry on their work in relative freedom from any disturbance.

2. No serious inroads in Germany's work-force were required, and her transportation network was undisturbed.

3. The raw materials allocated to the Luftwaffe were still intact, i.e. had not yet been destroyed by enemy air attack or captured by the enemy.

4. The destruction, by the enemy, of German aircraft on the ground was a rare occurrence.

5. Aircraft damage by inadequately-trained crews was far less common than was later to be the case.

6. Military operations were either at a standstill or were taking place far beyond the borders of the Reich.

In short, although these were war years, they were also years in which the aircraft industry could have exploited the advantages of near peacetime conditions.

And in spite of all this, production was pitifully small. The fault lies clearly with the Technical Office, whose lack of initiative cannot be ignored, and with the Luftwaffe General Staff (including its Chief, Jeschonnek*), which failed completely to provide the guidance expected of it.

---

*Preliminary investigation in the case against Generals Ploch, Reidenback and Tschersich, carried out by the Judge Advocate General, Dr. A. Kraell, revealed conclusively that the General Staff, including General Staff Chief Jeschonnek, was woefully lacking in unity and sense of direction as far as armament was concerned. (Based on oral information received from Dr. Kraell on 27 June 1955 as well as on the written record by Dr. Roeder, who served at that time as Court Martial Counsel; C/I/2, Karlsruhe Document Collection.)

Lest we be tempted to think that it was Germany's irrevocable fate to fall behind in air armament, as is indicated by the production figures for the period 1939-1941, let us turn to consideration of Milch's period of service as Chief of Luftwaffe Procurement and Supply. His first act after taking office was the establishment of definite production goals and in 1942, after the short period of decrease made inevitable by the unproductive confusion which he inherited, he managed to achieve a considerable increase in production over the previous year. In 1943, without neglecting bomber production, he pushed fighter production figures to a new high. Production planning for 1944 envisioned 4,000 fighter aircraft per month in comparison with Udet's average of 250 per month in 1941.*

And all of this Milch achieved during a period when:

1. Germany's home air defense was falling apart.

2. German aircraft factories, one after the other, were being attacked and were suffering heavy losses in materiel and in work force.

3. The destruction of raw materials through enemy air attack was becoming more and more common.

4. Working conditions in the factories were becoming more and more difficult.

5. The western, eastern, southern, and southeastern fronts, as a result of the territory lost during 1942, were coming closer and closer to Germany.

The production figures for the year 1944 were nothing less than heroic, but their tragedy was that they came "too late."

B. The Stoppage of Development

During the early stages of the war, as we have already pointed out, Germany, by failing to bring into play the mobilization measures designed for the eventuality of war, condemned herself to an eventual irrevocable numerical inferiority in the field of armaments.

_____

*The figure 250 refers to single-engine fighters only (Me-109's and FS-190's), not to twin-engine fighters, and only to new production. If we include the aircraft made available by conversion and repair, the figure is 330. Hardly an impressive figure in the midst of a war on several fronts!

In early 1940 this incomprehensible instance of neglect was followed by another blow--equally incomprehensible--which effectively prevented any further action on the part of the Luftwaffe and which robbed it of any chance it might have had of winning the armament race in time. It was the Technical Office in which this second blow originated. On 7 February 1940, General Udet requested approval for certain restrictions, as set forth in his letter to the Commander in Chief, Luftwaffe:[4]

> The present shortage of aluminum as well as of other nonferrous metals such as copper, tin, molybdenum, and chromium leaves me no choice but to recommend the following:
>
> I consider it imperative that everything possible be done to increase the production of those aircraft models which are in active use at the front. It is my opinion that a decrease in the production of aircraft models not in use at the front (i.e. training aircraft and reconnaissance machines), which could be replaced by converted single-engine and twin-engine fighters, can be justified for the near future.
>
> This change in our production program would result in a shift within the over-all production to those models chiefly in use at the front.

Two days later, on 9 February, a meeting was held under Goering's chairmanship (presumably in his function as chairman of the Ministers' Council for the Defense of the Reich). Among those present were Generaloberst Wilhelm Keitel, Generaloberst Milch, and Reichs Minister Funk. The following appears in the minutes of the meeting:[5]

> The Reichsmarschall announced as policy new instructions to the effect that the materiel resources presently on hand will be utilized to the maximum in order to produce as much armament equipment as possible within the shortest possible time. This takes precedence over previous instructions to conserve our available stocks of raw materials. <u>Those projects slated for completion in 1940 or 1941 at the latest will receive priority.</u>* Projects

---

*Underlining in original document.

of longer range than this will be approved only
within the framework of the Krauch Plan, designed
to insure our ultimate independence of the necessity
of importing materials from abroad. All other long-
range programs will be reevaluated carefully. Re-
assessment of our present areas of main effort in
the armament program, such as has already been
carried out by the Luftwaffe in its recommendation
to discontinue the production of certain aircraft
models, will be of paramount importance.

Unless we construe the reference to "long-range programs" as such
(and this interpretation is hardly justified), there is no specific
mention of any "stoppage of development" in the above record.* Some-
where else, however, the minutes must have contained explicit instructions to the aircraft industry, forbidding it to carry on further
developmental work on its own initiative. "The development of new aircraft models was systematically throttled by order of the Reichs Air
Ministry, which considered such development to be of secondary importance, 'because it could not be expected to bear tangible fruit before
the war was over.'"[6]

Surprisingly enough, there are no documents on record which shed
any light on the question of whether Goering acted on his own initiative
or whether the new policy merely represented official confirmation of
certain instructions already issued to the aircraft industry. There
is much mention of a stoppage of development, and presumably its consequences were of vital significance, but no one seems able to provide
any detailed information concerning it. Generalleutnant a. D. Erich
Schneider, for example, even places it at the wrong time when he states,
"In the fall of 1940 Hitler issued what was certainly one of the most
senseless orders of all time. Developmental work on all Wehrmacht
equipment which could not be promised for use at the front within one
year was to be stopped."[7]

The Fuehrer Directive of 11 September 1941,[8] the general text of
which is already familiar to us and which was implemented by General
Keitel in a detailed summary of instructions to the Wehrmacht High
Command under date of 10 October 1941, deals chiefly with procurement.
Keitel's instructions call for careful appraisal of the areas in which
procurement effort was to be concentrated and make it clear that procurement policy was to be based in part on the ability of industry to

_____

*Although von <u>Rohden</u> does speak of such.

51

deliver. A stoppage of development is mentioned only once, in the sentence "In order that these measures may be carried out effectively, I direct that all Wehrmacht requests for the procurement and development of equipment be forwarded to the appropriate procurement agencies through the office of the Chief, Wehrmacht High Command." Keitel's instructions continue, "The Chief, Wehrmacht High Command, will be responsible for evaluating each request, together with the Reichs Minister for Armament and Ammunition, in order to determine its feasibility and to decide, as my representatives, the type and scope of the contract to be awarded." Thus, the Chief, Wehrmacht High Command, is authorized "to prescribe curtailment of nonessential projects advanced by individual Wehrmacht branches. In the event that a certain project can be carried out only through the curtailment of other, more urgent programs, I /i.e. Keitel/ shall make the appropriate decision personally."

In a publication dated 8 January 1942, the Commander in Chief, Luftwaffe, adapted the Fuehrer Directive and Keitel's instructions into a special order applicable to the Luftwaffe.[9] Goering gives developmental work a good deal more scope than was implied in the first two orders. He points out the necessity for "more careful guidance of the Luftwaffe development program. The presentation of contemplated development programs to the Wehrmacht Armament Office, 'as was required by Keitel's order,' is no longer necessary. The State Secretary and Inspector General, Luftwaffe, however, is required to evaluate all development projects in terms of their feasibility as regards the current status of raw materials and production capacity."

The State Secretary was also empowered "to take any organizational measures necessary to the accomplishment of this order and to issue any instructions he deems appropriate." No such instructions have come to light so far. From the material at hand--the Fuehrer Directive, Keitel's order, and Goering's decree--we cannot deduce any systematic stoppage of development. Goering's decree states clearly that "if air armament or the conduct of air warfare will be influenced materially by any restrictive measures,"* such measures are to be reported in advance to the Chief, Luftwaffe General Staff.

Objectively considered, these documents do not in any way justify our speaking of a general stoppage of development. There were, of course, individual instances in which development was halted on the general basis of the four directives cited. We have already heard the

_____

*The underlining in the Goering decree was copied from the von Rohden documents.

Messerschmitt version of what happened in the case of the Me-262.

Feldmarschall Milch has the following to say in connection with the stoppage of development:[10]

> It is still quite clear in my memory that Hitler
> was interested only in calling a halt on those devel-
> opmental projects (in which he included research
> programs*) which could not possibly be completed in
> time to be of any use during the war. This is the
> way in which I interpreted his instructions in my
> capacity as Chief of Procurement and Supply, as the
> record of development of the Messerschmitt jet
> fighter and, above all, of the V-1 rocket (which
> was not ready for use until the summer of 1942)
> clearly indicate. The number of developmental
> projects carried on by the various Wehrmacht
> branches after the so-called "stop" was very con-
> siderable; these projects were continued with Hit-
> ler's permission and approval. Goering's attitude
> in the matter agreed closely with Hitler's, and his
> active role was restricted in general to the further
> transmittal of Hitler's expressed opinions.
>
> During his conversations with me, Hitler often
> mentioned his fear that highly-qualified technical
> personnel and valuable raw materials were being
> expended on projects which were admittedly interest-
> ing but had very little to do with winning the war.
> As an example, the Navy secretly prevailed upon the
> Messerschmitt Works to develop and build tropical
> barracks of duraluminum (which, incidentally, was
> Luftwaffe property), so that it would have termite-
> proof billets available when the time came to occupy
> the recovered German colonies. The construction of
> the aircraft carrier "Graf Zeppelin" and the develop-
> ment of certain highly-specialized artillery pieces
> were also cases in point.

---

*If Milch's statement is not the result of faulty recollection, it invites contemplation of an area of endeavor in which costly and far-reaching errors could be made, since it was administered exclusively by Referenten (junior staff officers assigned to specialized projects).

It is my feeling that some of the reproaches
which have been directed at our handling of this
phase of armament since 1945 are unjustified.

This serves to illustrate the care which should be exercised in
utilizing the term "stoppage of development."* So far, this term has
been used much too loosely so that it has degenerated into a glib
cliche.

C. The Establishment of Priorities

Until 1939 it was the responsibility of the Director of the Four-
Year Plan to distribute the Reich's resources among interested applicants, i.e. the various branches of the Wehrmacht as well as nonmilitary
applicants. The Luftwaffe had always been able to achieve a fairly
high priority rating, partly because the Commander in Chief, Luftwaffe,
and the Director of the Four-Year Plan were one and the same person,
and partly because the Army's requirements were so modest.

This situation changed rapidly as soon as the Wehrmacht High Command was entrusted with the allocation of resources and the exigencies
of war gave rise to more significant demands on the part of the Army
High Command. The Navy, traditionally all else but modest in its requests, was also driven to increased requirements as the submarine war
became more and more acute. For a while, to be sure, the Luftwaffe was
able to hold on to its favorable priority, at least as far as preferred
production for the Ju-88 was concerned; however, once victory in the
West was a foregone conclusion, the Luftwaffe was demoted to fifth place
on the priority scale,[11] despite the fact that the Battle of Britain was
yet to come. Hitler, of course, was already completely absorbed in his
plans for Russia, and it was obvious that the German Army would have

---

*On the basis of statements by Major a. D. (Lt. Col.?) Halder
(former Chief of Antiaircraft Rocket Development in Peenemuende) in
Flakentwicklung-Flakraketen, 1945 (Development in the Field of Antiaircraft Artillery and Antiaircraft Rockets), for example, the contention
that the stoppage of development resulted in a delay of two years in
the construction of the antiaircraft rocket seems to be without foun-
dation, although it is advanced by an acknowledged expert in the field,
General der Flak a. D. von Axthelm. The statements made by Colonel
a. D. Rudolf Bree, who accuses Halder of having obstructed the development of the antiaircraft rocket during 1941 and 1942, are not convincing.
(Statements of all three (Bree, Halder and von Axthelm) are on file in
C/VI/1b, Karlsruhe Document Collection.)

to be expanded considerably if his plans were to be realized. Forty new divisions would have to be formed and equipped, and under these circumstances there was no doubt but that the Army's requirements would have to come ahead of those of the Luftwaffe and the Navy. As Hitler explained to the Commander in Chief, Army,[12] once the lightning campaign had been brought to victorious conclusion, fifty or sixty divisions would be sufficient to occupy those parts of Russia which Hitler hoped to bring under his sway. It would then be possible to disband a part of the land force and to utilize the manpower thus freed in armament work in behalf of the Luftwaffe and the Navy.

Even before the end of 1941, it was obvious that Hitler's plans were going awry. Instead of surrendering at Moscow, the Russians pushed on in a series of attacks against the hard-pressed German Army Group Center. As a result, the projected release of large contingents of manpower for utilization by the Luftwaffe and the Navy never came to pass. On the contrary, it was more imperative than ever that the production of armored equipment for the Army be increased to the utmost. The problem of replacing the high materiel losses sustained by the Army during the Russian winter understandably took first priority.

To be sure, with the revised priority table issued by the Chairman of the Reichs Defense Council, Reichsmarschall Goering, (in concurrence with the Reichs Ministry for Armament and Ammunition[13]) on 7 February 1941,[14] two new special classifications were added; "S" and--even higher--"SS," and the Luftwaffe was given "SS" rating for the production of all vitally important aircraft models. In addition, the "SS" rating was assigned to work in progress on experimental models of the Ju-252, Ju-288, Me-161, Me-321, FW-191, DFS-331, and Go-242 types and to the production of Luftwaffe ammunition, antiaircraft artillery, aiming sights, and searchlights. A number of other important projects were included in the "S" category.

Thus, Luftwaffe armament activity managed to retain a certain degree of independence, both under Dr. Fritz Todt and under Albert Speer. Allocation of raw materials, however, was becoming more and more exclusively the prerogative of the Reichs Ministry for Armament and Ammunition, and it is natural that the Ministry tended to favor the Army and the Navy, neither of which had shown itself so aggressively independent as the Luftwaffe. And once Hitler assumed command of the Army (after the resignation of its Commander in Chief, Generalfeldmarschall von Brauchitsch) and came into more direct personal contact with the desperate situation on the Eastern front, it was naturally the Army--whose plight was continually before his eyes--which claimed the greatest share of his attention. A close second was the Navy with its submarines, by means of which he hoped to achieve the victory over England which the Luftwaffe had failed to bring in 1940.

As a matter of fact, it was not until 1944, when the Luftwaffe finally capitulated to Speer by setting up a fighter aircraft staff and abolishing the office of the Chief of Procurement and Supply, that it was able to obtain top priority for its fighter program and for the transfer of its armament works underground. Inevitably, we are tempted to wonder whether the Luftwaffe might not have been better off if it had given up its independence in armament activity at a far earlier date.

By the time the Luftwaffe agreed to subordinate itself to Speer, Germany's air cover had already fallen to pieces. The enemy enjoyed uncontested air supremacy, and the products of the enormous increase in armament activity which took place in 1944 were destined to land on the rubbish heap.

II - How the Luftwaffe Dissipated its Medium-Range Bomber Force in Close-Support Operations.*

In July 1939, in time for the campaign in Poland, the office of the Special Duty Air Commander was established as an operations staff for close-support actions.[15] General Freiherr von Richthofen, a veteran of the Spanish campaigns with the Condor Legion, was selected to head this office. The units assigned to General von Richthofen were those which had shown particular promise in close-support actions, chiefly dive-bomber, twin-engine, and ground-support aircraft units.

In Southern Poland, General von Richthofen was given command of all operations designed to furnish direct and indirect support for the

---

*Editor's Note: The Luftwaffe's emphasis of tactical air warfare over strategic air warfare is generally understood. Less well known, however, is that during the decisive Russian campaign the emphasis, within the field of tactical air warfare, was placed on close-support operations. This had a twofold result: medium-range bomber aircraft and their crews, equipped and trained for interdiction and short-range operations, were committed and wasted on close-support missions; and conversely, the Luftwaffe's close-support air effort in Russia was never what it could have been had enough suitable equipment and crews been available. Thus, while we assume that the Germans employed the wrong theory of air warfare in Russia, its wrongness was not proved because the means to test this theory were unavailable. In the following section Professor Suchenwirth examines the concomitants of the multiple failure.

56

ground forces, and it was chiefly due to his efforts that the campaign
in Poland came to a successful end so quickly. It was his energetic
intervention, for example, which served to obviate the development of
a serious crisis within the sphere of action of the Tenth Army. His
action was given official recognition by General von Reichenau, Commander in Chief of the Tenth Army, in the following message, dated
17 September:[16]

> Dear General von Richthofen: I should like to
> express my sincere thanks and grateful appreciation
> to you and to the units under your command for the
> effective support rendered to the Tenth Army during
> the battle of Sochaczew. I myself was a witness
> on several occasions to the extreme effectiveness
> and accuracy of the operations carried out by your
> units. It is my personal conviction that our victory
> could not have been so complete without the support
> of the Luftwaffe.

The VIII Air Corps, which came into being as a result of the group-
ing together of these ground-support units with the addition of a
fighter wing (the 27th) and a bomber wing (the 77th), repeatedly proved
itself worthy of the highest praise for its action during the campaigns
in France and Greece and finally for its role in the occupation of
Crete. The VIII Air Corps, in fact, may be termed one of the most important instruments of the German blitzkrieg technique. It was, after
all, the primary characteristic of blitzkrieg warfare that enemy resistance should be broken at the point of advance of the armored elements
by close-support air units, while the bombers prevented the enemy from
bringing reinforcements and supplies up to the battle field.

By concentrating their efforts at the focal point of the enemy
advance--a technique at which von Richthofen was a past master--,the
close-support forces could save their own advancing troops a good deal
of bloodshed and could guarantee a rapid push forward. The bomber units,
the so-called strategic element of the Luftwaffe, were thus freed for
commitment "against the larger, more tightly massed targets in the
enemy's rear area, such as, for example, the enemy communications
system."[17]

Any attempt on the part of Luftwaffe leaders to evaluate the experience gained thus far in terms of planning for future operations
was bound to be confronted with the decisive factor represented by the
VIII Air Corps. The results of the campaigns in Poland and France were

unmistakably clear in their implications. Beginning with the summer of 1940, however, Luftwaffe leaders were fully occupied with plans for the Russian campaign envisioned by Hitler. Hitler, as well as the Army High Command (which apparently raised no objections to his plan), was convinced that a blitzkrieg of no more than three to five months' duration would be sufficient to subdue Soviet Russia. The Commander in Chief, Luftwaffe, did indeed raise a number of objections to the plans devised by the Fuehrer; however, he failed to defend his point of view successfully and refused to accept the logical consequence, i.e. to resign from his post in protest after his objections had been brushed aside.

In accordance with Hitler's plan, the German Army, divided into three Army Groups, was to attack along a front more than 1,250 miles in length, in a theater of war which was naturally divided by the extensive Rokitno Swamps into three main areas, each of them containing an important military target (Leningrad, Moscow, and Kiev, the latter closely followed in importance by the cities of Kharkov and Rostov). The campaign in Poland had been directed against one main target only, Warsaw; the campaign in France, against the Channel coast and Paris.

At that time the strength of the one special duty air corps was sufficient to meet the needs of a concentration of ground effort against one main target. In view of the tremendously extensive operational area assigned to each of the three Army Groups in Russia, and taking into consideration the fact that successful penetration of the Eastern front was bound to create even more extensive operational areas as the German Army left western and central Europe behind and pushed on into the endless wastes of the Eurasian continent, there could be only one logical conclusion--to establish additional close-support air corps (or tactical Luftwaffe commands), at least so many that each Army Group would have one at its exclusive disposal. New activations of this type would have gone hand in hand with the consolidation of the bomber units into strategic air corps.

Fuehrer Directive #21 ("Barbarossa"), dated 18 December 1940,[18] and dealing with the campaign in Russia, envisioned two points of main effort as far as Luftwaffe operations were concerned. It forbade any attack on the Soviet armament industry "during the main operations," so that "all forces could be marshalled for action against the enemy air forces and for direct support of the ground forces." This indicates full awareness of the fact that the Luftwaffe, once it had fulfilled its primary objective of subduing the Russian Air Force, would have to provide direct (and no doubt indirect, as well) support for the German ground forces, and this for the duration of the hoped-for "lightning" campaign. The Luftwaffe, as it well knew, had no choice but to accept this mission as a necessary evil; we cannot give credence to the theory that the Luftwaffe was thrust into close-support operations on the spur of the moment and without any preparation whatsoever. On the contrary, Hitler made it perfectly clear from the very beginning that direct support of the Army would be an important Luftwaffe mission throughout the entire Russian campaign--for this is the significance of the phrase "main operations." The only unforeseen complication was the fact that the Russian campaign did not turn out to be a short one, but lasted until the downfall of Hitler's empire.

We may assume, then, that the Luftwaffe was fully aware of the type of performance expected of it, and this no later than 18 December 1940 (in all likelihood even earlier, since Luftwaffe leaders must have had a hand in the preparation of the Fuehrer Directive). In view of the experience gathered during the campaigns in Poland, France, and Greece, Luftwaffe leaders should certainly have realized, from the moment that Hitler informed them of his plan to attack Russia, that close-support operations would be required.

In short, the Luftwaffe had sufficient time for the planning, organizational, training, and procurement programs needed to fit it for its new mission. The Commander in Chief, Luftwaffe, was certainly informed of the plans for a Russian campaign no later than the Commander in Chief, Army. (This was on 21 July 1940 in Berlin,[19] when von Brauchitsch mentioned to Halder that the conference took place "under the usual circumstances." This gives us no clue as to whether or not Goering was present, but it is quite unlikely that he was.) Considering the fact that the relationship between Hitler and Goering was very close during that period, we may assume that Goering was aware of the plans for Russia at a much earlier date. Further, it can be taken for granted that Goering passed on this information, in strictest confidence, to his General Staff Chief, Jeschonnek.*

---

*General Hoffmann von Waldau, Chief of the Luftwaffe Operations Staff, expressed his concern regarding a possible Russian campaign to Admiral Wilhelm Moessl as early as the autumn of 1940. (Based on verbal information given to the author on 3 Sept 1954).

According to the Armed Forces Historian, Helmuth Greiner, "Hitler seems to have confided his plans to the Commander in Chief, Luftwaffe, at an early date, since it was apparent that the Luftwaffe Operations Staff was already aware of them by 8 August when it requested the Army

Thus Luftwaffe leaders had a good ten months in which to prepare their forces for the inevitable conflict with Soviet Russia, a conflict whose outcome--whether favorable or unfavorable--was bound to have tremendous significance for the fate of Germany. Their first step clearly should have been the firm organization of the new tactical Luftwaffe commands on a basis which would permit their immediate and smooth activation when the time came. This would have required early selection and training of the officers who were to be in charge of the new mission, concentration on the pilot training program for single-engine aircraft, and, last but by no means least, a timely increase in the production of single-engine machines, even if it meant using up the last materiel resources available; for it was obvious that at least three new tactical commands, with a number of new close-support wings (i.e. dive bombers and ground support aircraft), would have to be activated and equipped. Existing difficulties, including the Luftwaffe's relatively low priority for the allocation of raw materials, would simply have to have been overcome somehow.* This first step, however, was never taken. Instead, faced with the demands bound to arise out of a campaign against Soviet Russia, Luftwaffe leaders placed their reliance on half-measures.

High Command to provide certain information relative to the establishment of a Luftwaffe ground organization in the East. The Commander in Chief, Navy, on the other hand, was apparently not taken into Hitler's confidence until late September. . ." (Helmuth Greiner, Die oberste Wehrmachtfuehrung 1939-43 (The Top-Level Armed Forces Command from 1939 through 1943), (Wiesbaden, 1951), p. 295.)

*One might be tempted to treat this as one of those glib phrases so often utilized to excuse failure or neglect during wartime. However, it must be remembered that the Technical Office, under the supervision of State Secretary Milch after Udet's death, had actually managed to achieve a tremendous increase in armament production, an increase which was almost unbelievable in view of the Reich's situation at that time, and all without any alteration in the Luftwaffe's previous priority classification. If Luftwaffe leaders had insisted upon a further increase in the production of close-support aircraft, it probably would have led to earlier clarification of the relationship of the Technical Office to the Quartermaster General. And if this increase, upon which the General Staff ought to have insisted, had actually been achieved, Milch might have been appointed Chief of Luftwaffe Procurement and Supply as early as 1940. This would have been a decided advantage as far as Luftwaffe armament was concerned.

The VIII Air Corps was the only real close-support unit available.* The other air corps assigned to the Eastern front (the IV, V, II, and I) had been given the mission of providing direct support for the Army, but had not been issued the equipment necessary to fulfill this mission.

As we can tell from the organizational chart of the Fourth Air Fleet,[20] neither the IV nor the V Air Corps had any dive bombers at its disposal. The IV Air Corps, with four bomber and three single-engine fighter groups, was comparatively weak to begin with. The V Air Corps had eight bomber and three single-engine fighter groups. The Second Air Fleet, in addition to the VIII Air Corps (with three bomber, five and one-third dive-bomber, two twin-engine fighter, three single-engine fighter, and one air transport group), also had at its disposal the II Air Corps, with its five bomber, three dive-bomber, two close-support (Me-110), and one air transport group. The First Air Fleet, assigned to the northern sector of the Eastern front, had no dive bombers whatsoever, but only eight bomber and three and one-third single-engine fighter groups.╱

Thus it was only the Second Air Fleet, with its two Air Corps, which was adequately equipped for close-support operations. The Fourth and First Air Fleets, on the other hand, were forced to employ their bomber (the First Air Fleet had only the vulnerable Ju-88; the Fourth

---

*Even the assignment of the Bombardment Wing Richthofen was, in a sense, a violation of principle.

╱During the latter course of operations there were, naturally, alterations in the materiel make-up of the Air Fleets and Air Corps. On 10 August 1941, for example, the Second Air Fleet had four bomber, one dive-bomber, one close-support, and four fighter groups; by 10 October, during its employment in the battles of Bryansk and Vyaz'ma, it had reached its peak strength, with seven and two-thirds bomber, five dive-bomber, two close-support, six fighter, and three air transport groups. On 1 November 1941 the IV Air Corps, Fourth Air Fleet, in the midst of the heavy fighting on the Crimea and near Rostov, had the following forces at its disposal: six bomber, three dive-bomber, and four fighter groups. Similarly, the First Air Fleet, while engaged in the operations leading to the encirclement of Leningrad, was temporarily assigned the VIII Air Corps and had, in addition, the following forces in its own I Air Corps: eleven bomber, two twin-engine fighter, and three single-engine fighter groups (status on 2 September 1941). By 1 December, unfortunately right in the midst of the Russian counter-offensive at Tikhvin, I Air Corps strength had been reduced to four bomber and three single-engine fighter groups. (F/I/1d, Karlsruhe Document Collection.)

was a bit better off--the IV Air Corps was completely equipped with the more robust He-111 and the V Air Corps had two wings of Ju-88's and one of He-111's) and single-engine fighter aircraft in ground-support operations, all of them machines which could not land just anywhere with impunity.

In addition, in low-altitude flight (which was often necessary in this type of operation) the heavy bombers presented a far better target than their lighter, single-engine counterparts for the implacable Russians, who were wont to let fire with everything they had. In view of the size of the crews and the cost and time which had gone into their training and the amount of materiel and armament carried, the loss of a heavy bomber was more painfully felt than that of a light close-support aircraft. Then, too, the heavy bombers were far more vulnerable to damage while landing on the often unsuitable airfields in the East than were the Ju-87's and Hs-123's.

Even the He-111's were not ideal for close-support operations, but in spite of this they were utilized in air transport missions to Demjansk and Stalingrad. The losses incurred were correspondingly high. During the air supply operations to Stalingrad alone, 165 He-111's--more than one entire bomber wing--were destroyed.[21]

The result, quite simply, was a continuing wear and tear on bomber aircraft on the Eastern front, due entirely to their being employed in a type of operation for which they were not suited. The losses incurred could have been avoided to a very large extent if Luftwaffe leaders had been wise enough to insist upon an increase in the production of single-engine bombers in 1940. Such an increase could have been balanced by a temporary decrease in the manufacture of heavy bombers, and--considering the lower rate of loss with lighter bombers (a factor which could and should have been foreseen)--the final result would have been more favorable.

The facts which confront us defy understanding. The Luftwaffe General Staff had already seen, in Spain, the decided advantages to be gained from the tactical employment of air forces and had even taken steps to establish a special force for close-support operations. This is evidenced by the activation of the V Special Duty Air Command in 1939 and its later expansion into the VIII Air Corps. These actions occurred during the course of the campaigns in Poland and in France; and in both instances, the Luftwaffe was commited in only one, limited theater of operations. In 1941, however, when the Soviet theater of operations-- with its enormous geographic extent--began to spread out, at a time when fighting was going on in the Mediterranean theater and when the West and Germany herself were being subjected to British terror raids,--in short, when the war had spread to a number of separate fronts--German military leaders contented themselves with reinforcing only one Air Corps (the IId) with additional close-support forces. Moreover, the difficulties created in command channels as a result of this particular action are clearly evidenced by the fact that it was found necessary to appoint a special close-support commander within the II Air Corps to take care of the single-engine bomber forces (because of the total lack of uniformity in the equipment issued).

The Luftwaffe was resigned to the necessity of providing direct support for the Army ground forces, as, indeed, it had to be in view of the fact that the plight of the German armies had become steadily worse since their defeat at Stalingrad and also as a result of unrealistic orders from the Fuehrer to hold indefensible areas. After all, it was a matter of saving German soldiers and holding back the Soviet avalanche. Unfortunately, for the forces assigned to close-support operations as well as for the outcome of the entire war, the measures taken in regard to organization and equipment were no more than half-measures. The General Staff, the brain of the Luftwaffe, had failed to think through to its logical conclusion the thought which inspired the creation of the VIII Air Corps.

Chapter 3

THE CRITICAL BATTLES AND TURNING POINTS OF THE WAR

I - The Battle of Britain

The German Air Force, which had gained a reputation for invincibility during three campaigns, had, as a matter of fact, failed to perform really adequately during the last phase of the third of these campaigns; namely during the battle for air supremacy at Dunkirk. There, it had missed its goal, the destruction of the British Army, partly as a result of the fight put up by the Spitfires and partly as a result of unfavorable weather conditions and the over-ambitious scope of the mission. Dunkirk, however, was a single episode, its memory soon blotted out by Luftwaffe successes during the campaign in France. Moreover, the unfavorable aspects of the Dunkirk operation, which could and should have provided food for serious thought, were overshadowed by the memory of the wealth of enemy materiel covering the length of the beach, left behind by an army which was forced to embark too hastily to take along the greater part of its weapons, tanks, motor vehicles, and other equipment.

While the commitment of the Luftwaffe at Dunkirk was the result of a direct, spur-of-the-moment offer which Goering made to Hitler,[1] it can hardly be said that the Reichsmarschall was equally enthusiastic about Directive 17, of 1 August 1940,[2] which was passed on to him by the Commander in Chief, Wehrmacht, and which referred to the Luftwaffe's role in the "conduct of air and sea warfare against England." General Kammhuber[3] maintains that Goering's lack of enthusiasm for Directive 17 is clearly visible in the wording of his Instructions for the Air War against England[4] of 30 June 1940.

By intensifying air warfare against England, Hitler hoped to bring the British leaders to the point where they would be willing to discuss peace. What he wanted was an honorable peace, one which would pave the way to a lasting understanding between the two countries. In this way he would have had his hands free for the Russian campaign, plans for which were already under way.

Just how strong was the German Luftwaffe at this point? On 3 August 1940, according to the records of the Quartermaster General, the authorized single-engine fighter aircraft strength stood at 1,171; actual strength was 1,065, and of these 878 (comprising ten single-engine

64

fighter wings with a total of twenty-eight groups) were combat-ready. Two of these ten wings (a total of six groups), to be sure, were tied to home air defense operations,[5] so that the number of single-engine fighter aircraft available at the beginning of the Battle of Britain was reduced to 760. At the same time, the Luftwaffe had three wings (eight groups) of twin-engine fighter aircraft. The authorized strength was 332 machines, the actual strength 310, of which 240 were in a state of combat readiness. It must be emphasized that this was aircraft strength only; there were not enough trained crews available to man the aircraft on hand. Thus, effective twin-engine fighter strength (i.e. fully manned aircraft) was probably about 230. According to the Quarter-master General reports, authorized bomber strength stood at 1,638 on 3 August; actual strength was 1,458, 818 of which were combat-ready. Of the latter, however, (a total of fifteen bomber wings or forty-two groups), two wings--or six groups--were based in Norway and therefore could have intervened effectively under only very special circumstances. In other words, of the total of 823 bombers, the Second and Third Air Fleets had an average of 700-800 at their disposal during the first two months of the Battle of Britain. The dive bombers were represented in an authorized strength of 429 aircraft and an actual strength of 446; in reality, 343 were available for action on 3 August. In addition, on 20 September, an experimental fighter-bomber group (the II Close-Support Group, 2d Training Wing) equipped with forty Me-109's, was sent into action for the first time.

British air strength at the beginning of the struggle was made up of sixty single-engine fighter squadrons, or a total of 960 aircraft. To be sure, these squadrons also had reserve forces upon which they could draw if necessary. Due to the fact that there were eight squadrons not prepared for immediate action, the actual strength on 7 August 1940 was 714 single-engine fighter aircraft. This number was subject to alteration during the various phases of the struggle (on 25 September, for example, it was down to 665). According to British data, losses during the period 11 August-28 September 1940 amounted to 669 single-engine fighter aircraft, while a total of 936 was produced during the same period. British bomber strength (actual strength as of 8 August 1940: 471 aircraft) played no role in the Battle of Britain.

By the end of September 1940, this strength ratio had altered so that 665 British single-engine fighters were facing a German force composed of 276 single-engine fighters, 130 fighter-bombers, 100 twin-engine fighters, 700-800 bombers, 343 dive bombers, and 26 close-support aircraft.

During the period 10 July-31 October 1940, German losses amounted to 1,733 bombers and single-engine fighters, while the British lost 915 single-engine fighters.[6] In terms of personnel, the German losses were far more critical than the British ones, since the fighting took place over British territory. When a German aircraft was shot down, her crew--assuming that it was able to escape from the damaged airplane-- was immediately taken prisoner and was this irrevocably lost to Germany. These losses were augmented by the ones incurred through crashes into the English Channel, where rescue operations were often impossible. Quartermaster General records indicate German losses for the period 3 August-28 September 1940 as 719 bomber aircraft (total destruction and 10% or more damage) and 400 crews. (For the dive bombers, the figures are 97 machines and 61 crews.) When British aircraft were downed, on the other hand, there was a much greater chance that their crews could be salvaged for future reassignment to other aircraft; they were not permanently lost to future operations. The situation for German single-engine and twin-engine fighter crews, of course, was the same as that described above in connection with the bomber crews.

In view of the figures given above, it is clear that the production of aircraft and the training of crews to man them was a key problem for Germany. During 1940 a total of 11,376 aircraft was produced in Germany (this includes new production, conversion of older models, and repair), as reflected in Quartermaster General reports; this total included 2,268 Me-109 fighters, 1,114 Me-110 fighters, 2,741 bombers (all types), and 480 dive bombers.

In evaluating the course of the Battle of Britain, a comparison of the number of fighter aircraft produced by each side during 1940 is significant. The 3,382 single-engine and twin-engine fighter aircraft reflected in the Luftwaffe's Quartermaster General records correspond to 4,283 fighters produced by the British during the same year. This very revealing figure provides ample proof of England's greater strength in the field of air armament. When we bear in mind that the German fighters, tied to the bombers they escorted, were unable to maneuver with complete freedom and were thus more vulnerable to enemy action than they otherwise would have been, the production fugures given above might just as well be considered decisive. During the month of August, a period of intensive fighting, the German aircraft industry produced 160 Me-109's and 114 Me-110's, a total of 274 new fighter aircraft (together with the aircraft released from repair, the total for the month was 301--222 Me-109's and 79 Me-110's), while the British produced 476. This is particularly interesting when we consider that the British began the year with a production figure of 157 aircraft (for January) and Germany with a figure of 136 (Me-109's and Me-110's together); thus Britain succeeded in trebling her production during the year, while Germany barely doubled hers.[7] Moreover, the import of American aircraft served to weight the numerical balance in Britain's favor.*

If we exclude the twin-engine fighters, and base our comparison on the number of single-engine fighters alone, then the ratio is even less favorable for Germany. The 2,268 Me-109's reflected in Quartermaster General records for 1940 are balanced by 4,283 British single-engine fighters; a ratio of nearly 1:2.

As far as personnel losses ere concerned, we must not lose sight of the fact that it was the highly-qualified, peacetime-trained crews who were affected first. And the new crop of bomber pilots coming from the flight schools was no longer so well-trained in instrument flight, partly because the Ju-52's assigned to the Chief of Training were continually being loaned out for special missions.⧸

Appraisal of the British-German strength ratio and of the opportunities for development available to both sides would seem to substantiate the conclusion of the military author, Dr. Theo Weber in the Swiss journal, Flugwehr und Technik: "It is clear that the Luftwaffe simply did not have the means of solving this problem in the autumn of 1940."[8] Germany did not possess the long-range, heavy bombers which might have struck a decisive blow against the sources of the enemy's military strength. The wrong decision of 29 April 1937 was making itself felt.

The goal of forcing England to the point of peace negotiations was not attained during a single phase of the intensified air warfare carried out by the Luftwaffe during the period 8 (or 13) August 1940 to early June 1941. It was not, however, the high losses inflicted by Britain's undeniably efficient air defenses which forced the Luftwaffe to withdraw from the battle; it was rather the fact that the date which Hitler had selected (almost at the same time as he ordered intensification of the air war with England) for the launching of the campaign against Soviet Russia was drawing near, and he was still convinced that Russia would have to be subdued if Germany were to be safe.

One other factor came to England's aid, the advent of the proverbial British autumn weather on 16 September 1940. The two months which

---

*By 3 September 1940, the United States had delivered a total of 3,633 aircraft to England (Payne, L. G. S., Air Dates, Heinemann, (London, 1957), p. 110).

⧸See above, Chapter 1.

Hitler had waited, in the hope that Britain would capitulate, now took their toll.

The German attackers were handicapped in other ways as well. The Luftwaffe had no ground control system for the ground-to-air guidance of fighter aircraft, whereas the British had a well-functioning one at their disposal. This was compensated for to some extent, however, by the efficiency of the German radio monitoring service.

The British also had a tremendous advantage in their radar equipment, which had been under development since 1936 in the National Physics Research Institute, chiefly at the instigation of the Scotsman Robert Watson Watt, who had recognized its significance in time and whose work had been most generously supported. The radar instruments set up along the English coast ranged over the coastal waters and sometimes even as far as the Luftwaffe assembly areas, so that the approach of enemy aircraft could be detected well in advance. Early warning made it possible for the British fighters to intercept the enemy in plenty of time, which, of course, could not have been the case without the help of radar. In addition, British home air defense operations were superbly organized and administered. Unfortunately, the Luftwaffe High Command made no serious attempt to destroy the British coastal radar stations by bombardment, or even to keep them under continuous harrassing attack. After 15 August there were no more German attacks on these stations. Five stations had been bombed and damaged, but none had been destroyed completely. Actually, the number of aircraft employed (one bomb-carrying twin-engine fighter group from the Second Air Fleet with twelve Me-110's and eight Me-109's) was not really sufficient for such a mission. As Kammhuber says, "The enemy was continually peeking at our cards - and it was our own fault!"[9] This was also the reason why no prospectively successful attacks could be undertaken against the British ground organization. At Christmas 1940, the British placed their first panoramic-view radar equipment at the disposal of the night fighter control organization. As a result, the night fighters, hitherto completely helpless, soon began to chalk up records of German aircraft downed. The figure for March was twenty-two, for April twenty, and for May allegedly one hundred. In any case, German air supremacy at night, previously a foregone conclusion, was now seriously threatened. In addition, from March on British long-range fighter operations out over the Channel were highly successful.

*   *   *

It is not the purpose of the present study to go into the individual phases of the Battle of Britain in order to examine the

68

appropriateness of the decisions taken by command. We are far more interested in the question of whether and, if so, to what extent, the Battle of Britain can be termed a turning point.

In answering this question, we must bear in mind the fact that the Battle of Britain was broken off prematurely by order of top-level command because the German Air Force was needed for the forthcoming war with Soviet Russia. Operations against England were not discontinued because they were recognized as hopeless or because they could no longer be justified in terms of the losses incurred.

Still, it was the first time that the Luftwaffe had brought its main strength to bear in a large-scale operation of many weeks' duration without gaining its objective. For the fact remained that its goal had not been achieved. The myth of Luftwaffe invincibility had been exploded. England had been left in command of the battlefield, and had managed to maintain herself in the face of the sharp decline in morale occasioned by France's dropping out of the war.

And this was significant--particularly in point of morale. By no means, however, could it be viewed as a turning point after which nothing would ever again go right for the Luftwaffe. Even the depletion suffered in the ranks of Germany's best-trained crews was not sufficient to induce such a turning point. Newly recruited, younger crews had been gathering combat experience in the meantime, and during the two years to follow, (1941 and 1942) there is still no instance of out-and-out failure on the part of the Luftwaffe in any theater of operations.

Even so, the Battle of Britain does represent a turning point insofar as Germany failed to recognize and appreciate the reasons which had prevented the Luftwaffe from attaining its objective. These reasons are the following:

1. The lack of purposeful guidance in German air armament during the Udet period. At that time, when there was no appreciable difference in the quality of the German and British fighter aircraft, quantity played an important role. And Udet and his staff, primarily interested in the development of new models, failed entirely to recognize this fact. Germany should have kept herself systematically informed of the efficacy of the British air armament program and should have drawn the inevitable conclusions, chief of which was the need for a continuing increase in the production of aircraft. Germany's military leaders, soon to be confronted with the bitter seriousness of war with Russia, did not even find it necessary to take a closer look at Udet's office of Chief of Procurement and Supply with a view to getting armament

69

production up to wartime levels,* nor did they take steps (and this includes the expansion of training) to fill in the gaps left by the Battle of Britain. Thus, we are justified in treating the Battle of Britain as a turning point. As far as aircraft crews were concerned, the Luftwaffe had been eating into its capital; yet its leaders were unable to see the need for revitalizing the training program.

2. Prior to the Battle of Britain, Germany rashly underestimated the enemy's military strength. The Reichs Intelligence Service had drawn far too rosy a picture; the strength figures it worked out were

---

*Let us compare once more the production figures of the Udet era--16,665 in 1940 and 13,379 in 1941 (both figures include aircraft of all types)--with the figure achieved during the "year of catastrophe," 1944--44,738 aircraft!

In this connection see also the scathing evaluation of German intelligence by G. W. Feuchter. Feuchter states:

> With the beginning of the Battle of Britain, the Intelligence Branch, Luftwaffe Operations Staff, issued official daily situation reports, which were distributed not only to all higher-level operations staffs but also to the troop staffs. In addition to other information, these reports contained the number of aircraft downed by the Luftwaffe and, using this figure as a basis, estimated the number of fighter aircraft presumably still at the disposal of British home air defense operations for the day concerned. According to these reports, which, after all, represented "official" announcements by the Luftwaffe Operations Staff and served as a basis for deployment planning by the troop-level staffs, . . . the British fighter aircraft force should have been shot down in its entirety by the beginning of September 1940.

On page 170, Feuchter points out those results of the Battle of Britain which particularly affected the subsequent course of the war: Germany's failure to gain uncontested air supremacy by neutralizing the British air forces, with the result that the German armament industry could no longer develop unhindered; bolstering of the morale of the French civilian population; and strengthening the will to underground resistance on the part of the occupied countries. (Georg W. Feuchter, Geschichte des Luftkriegs (History of the Air War), (Bonn, 1954), pp 161, 170.)

woefully off. Underestimating enemy strength is clearly one of the most frequent causes of military failure. Germany's leaders could have profited by the admittedly unpleasant surprise they received, if they had determined then and there to err in the direction of overestimation of the strength of a potential enemy in the future, in order to be certain that their own preparations would be adequate. But was this the case? As far as Russia was concerned--and to a lesser extent also in the case of America--it most certainly was not.

With incomprehensible stubbornness, Germany's leaders continued to underestimate the military strength of their adversaries until the final catastrophe broke in upon them.

3. Failure to develop a long-range, heavy bomber (and this could have been only a four-engine bomber) capable of employment in strategic air warfare. Again, Germany failed to profit by her lesson. Right up to the time of his death, Udet was still experimenting with the tandem-engine system for the He-177, and even Milch, who inherited what was admittedly a miserable situation, could not bring himself to order a switch to four independently functioning engines until it was too late. Another instance in which the lessons of bitter experience went unheeded. The same thing also happened in the case of the long-range fighter, the unfortunate affair of the Me-210 taking place at about the same time.

4. The superiority of the British radar equipment. In spite of the valiant effort made by General Martini, of the Luftwaffe signal forces, the British had too much of a head start for Germany to catch up with them in time. As a matter of fact, the Luftwaffe, engaged from 1943 to the end of the war in a life-and-death struggle to protect the Reich, was never to have access to radar instruments which were invulnerable to jamming--and thus a match for the Anglo-American equipment--simply because the German radar industry was incapable of developing radar tubes for the lower centimeter wave ranges.

In a very real sense, the Battle of Britain was the handwriting on the wall. And neither Goering, Jeschonnek, nor Udet had been able to decipher it. If they had understood its significance, there would still have been time to correct the defects and to launch a new and more forceful attack against the West. For conflict with the West was inevitable until such time as the British wasps' nest could be burned out. It was to take a lot more writing on the wall, however, before the Luftwaffe's top-level leaders learned to read even a part of it. By the time that point had been reached, of course, it was already too late.

II - The War against Soviet Russia

The war against Soviet Russia clearly represented one of the most significant turning points for the Luftwaffe, as well as for the entire German Armed Forces. And all the important factors which made it so were present in its very beginning.

Since the German victory over France, there was only one enemy, England, to be faced in the West; to be sure, operations against England also required action on the high seas and, after 1940, in the Mediterranean as well. The decision to engage in war against Soviet Russia, however, meant the opening of a new and geographically enormous theater of operations. And for the first time since the end of the campaign in France, it was primarily a theater of Army and Luftwaffe operations. Army preparations for this new mission included the activation of a total of forty new divisions;10 this, in turn, represented an extremely heavy burden on Germany's armament industries. As a result, the Luftwaffe expansion originally planned for the same period had to be relegated to the background. Thus, while the Army was able to face the enemy in the East with a considerably strengthened force (still not strong enough, as events were to prove), reinforcement of Luftwaffe strength was limited to replacement of the losses entailed by the Battle of Britain.

If there was any justification for the momentous decision to start a war against Soviet Russia as a means of counteracting the potential threat of her entry into the European war, it could have been only the certainty that she could be conquered in another lightning campaign. But was this a certainty? It could be counted as such only if Germany were able, once again, to eliminate the danger of the time factor--as she had done in the campaigns in Poland, Norway, the West, and the Balkans (the latter campaign having been made necessary by Italy's boastful and bumbling intervention in Greece)--and this in an operational area of almost endless depth.

There were two ways in which the time factor might be fatal. In the first place, England, still too weak to continue offensive operations at the moment, was pushing armament production as rapidly as possible, and America, standing behind her, was becoming progressively more unfriendly. In the second place, Germany would not be in a position to attack until spring at the earliest (due to the Balkan campaign, the attack was not to begin until 22 June), and this would leave only a few months' time before the advent of the Russian winter, during which the Soviet giant would have time to recover his strength. If the time element could not be overcome by Germany, then the whole Russian campaign would be tantamount to stirring up a hornets' nest without having the means to destroy it.

From all possible viewpoints, then, the risk entailed was a serious one. If Germany should not succeed in making the Russian campaign into another glorious episode like her earlier campaigns, then she was bound to be in for a life-and-death struggle, for she would be engaged in a destruction-bringing war on several fronts at the same time. It was obvious that the demands of such a war would raise Army requirments tremendously, with the result that Luftwaffe and Navy needs would be engaged in an action which permitted no respite, in a country whose airfields were definitely substandard and whose climate was barbaric.

In other words, the majority of the Luftwaffe units (which were, of course, committed in Russia) faced the certain prospect of continual attrition and depletion. And the situation of those units remaining in the West was not a great deal better. How could they expect to meet the British offensive which began at the same time as the Russian campaign and which would soon be strengthened immeasurably by the entry of the United States into the war? What chance did the Luftwaffe have of meeting the requirements for increased air strength in the Mediterranean? Not even Army strength was put to such a demanding test by the opening of the Russian campaign. The Army was still waging war in Cyrenaica, and its continued occupation of Norway and France, while it tied up a considerable number of troops, could be carried out by troops which needed a rest and which could prepare themselves for renewed commitment at the front in a country whose occupation required no further military action. It was the Luftwaffe, the majority of whose forces were called directly from the Battle of Britain to operations against Soviet Russia, which faced the most serious problems.

In view of this fact, it was no wonder that it was the Commander in Chief, Luftwaffe, more than any other German military leader, who spoke out against Hitler's plans for a campaign against Soviet Russia. It cannot be denied that Goering had a certain intuition as far as political developments were concerned. And the fact that he, personally,-- as a conscientious husband and father, as possessor of valuable art collections, and as owner of a considerable amount of real estate--had a good deal more to lose than to gain from a new war, presumably served to sharpen his intuition. In any case, it was not the Commander in Chief, Army, who spoke up against the Russian campaign, but the Commander in Chief, Luftwaffe, Hitler's closest confidant.

Goering's warnings against a campaign in the East were even more vehement than those of the Commander in Chief, Navy. Raeder did his best to distract Hitler's attention from the East by attempting to persuade him that if Germany's position in the Near East could be made strong enough, a war with Russia would be unnecessary.

When Hitler told him of his plans for Russia, Goering requested time to think it over,[11] since he was somewhat surprised by Hitler's reasoning that it was imperative that Germany, "by means of a quick, tightly concentrated attack, . . . destroy" Russian military potential before America would be able to build up her armament and her forces. Goering states that he pleaded with Hitler on the evening of that same day "not to start a war with Russia, either then or in the near future." He begged Hitler to let the "danger represented by Russia remain in abeyance" for a while longer--after all, Hitler's genius had been responsible for the fact that Germany had had to wage war on only one front in the beginning. A conflict with Russia would mean the entry of a third world power in the war against Germany. Once more, Germany would stand alone against the whole world--and alone on two fronts for the neighboring states were inconsequential. Hitler pointed out that by 1942/43, which--according to the information available to him--was the earliest date at which Russia would be fully prepared for war, "Germany would have either beaten England or have come to terms with her. But a good many more Luftwaffe attacks were necessary before this could be brought about, and if Germany went to war against Russia, at least two thirds of Luftwaffe strength would have to be transferred to the East." Goering made the consequences clear to Hitler: "The sacrifices made so far by the Luftwaffe in its attacks on England would be in vain; the British aircraft industry would have time to recover; Germany would renounce certain sure victories (Suez, Gibraltar) and with them the possibility of reaching an 'agreement' with England and, thereby, of guiding Russia's armament activity into another channel."

According to another report,[12] Goering continued to "oppose Hitler's plan until the latter said to him: 'Goering, why don't you stop trying to persuade me to drop my plans for Russia? I've made up my mind!'"

Thus, the turning point for the Luftwaffe became inevitable. As Goering expressed it in his appeal to the Fuehrer, "My Fuehrer, the ultimate decision is yours to make. May God guide you and help you to prove your rightness in the face of opposition! I, myself, am forced to oppose your point of view in this respect. May God protect you! But please remember that I cannot be blamed if I am unable to carry out our plans for expanding the Luftwaffe!" Hitler replied, "You will be able to continue operations against England in six weeks," whereupon Goering pointed out that ". . . the Luftwaffe is the only Wehrmacht branch which has not had a breathing space since the war began. I told you when we first went to war that I was going into battle with my training squads, and now they're all gone." Furthermore, said Goering, "I'm not at all sure that you can beat Russia in six weeks. The ground forces can't fight any more without Luftwaffe support. They're always screaming for the Luftwaffe. There's nothing I'd like better than to have you proven right, but, frankly, I doubt that you will be."[13]

The Russian campaign began on 22 June 1941. Its very beginning represented a race against time. And by the advent of winter on the Soviet front (between 6 and 12 December 1941), after which the Russians began their counteroffensive, it was obvious that Germany had lost the race. The beginning of the Russian campaign was a race against time in another respect as well, and in this respect, too, Germany lost the race. On 11 December 1941, America officially declared war against Germany; in other words, Goering's fears became reality.

With the beginning of the Russian campaign, the Luftwaffe had a total of 2,000 aircraft in the East, broken down into twenty-nine and one-half bomber, nine and one-third dive-bomber, twenty single-engine fighter, two twin-engine fighter, and two close-support groups, and twelve long-range reconnaissance squadrons. To these must be added five air transport groups, with 150 aircraft, and eight liaison squadrons, with eighty aircraft. In addition, the Army had fourteen long-range reconnaissance squadrons (with 140 aircraft), forty-five short-range reconnaissance squadrons (with 450 aircraft), and eleven liaison squadrons (with 110 aircraft).[14]

The following Luftwaffe strength remained in the West or was engaged in home air defense operations:

In the West: (Third Air Fleet; 660 aircraft)

twelve and one-third bomber groups, six single-engine fighter groups, one and one-third twin-engine fighter groups, seven long-range reconnaissance squadrons.

In home air defense, Commander Center: (190 aircraft)

one and two-thirds single-engine fighter groups, four and two-thirds twin-engine fighter groups.

In the Mediterranean: (X Air Corps and Air Commander, Africa)

five bomber groups, three dive-bomber groups, one and one-third

75

single-engine fighter groups, one and one-third twin-engine fighter groups, five long-range reconnaissance squadrons.

In Norway: (Fifth Air Fleet, less those units employed in Russia)

one and .. -thirds bomber groups, one single-engine fighter group, four long-range reconnaissance squadrons.[15]

As we have seen, Germany's air strength was already fairly widely dissipated. She was engaged in warfare on several fronts.

Heretofore, the Luftwaffe had always been able to cover itself with glory because the duration of its actions and the conditions under which it was operating were such that its weaknesses (which we have already discussed) had no chance to take effect. During the Battle of Britain it had managed to hold its own in a hard fight; in Russia it was simply overwhelmed. The fact that there was no four-engine bomber which could reach and destroy the enemy's armament works (some of which were already located beyond the Ural Mountains), the scarcity of aircraft suitable for close-support operations, the lack of an adequate air transport fleet, the fact that air armament production had been far too small during 1939 and 1940 and had not been materially increased during 1941--all of these weaknesses began to make themselves felt as soon as the war became stationary or threatened to remain at the same stage of relentless, hard fighting.

Although the establishment of a reserve force was urgently necessary, now that war on several fronts had become a reality, it was, for that very reason an impossibility. Sudden requirements for reinforcements at individual sectors of the front could be met only by the expedient of withdrawing forces from other sectors, which, in turn, created dangerous gaps in the latter. Thus, once the urgent need for additional reinforcements in home air defense operations became acute, the fate of the Luftwaffe was sealed. The end result was bound to be a weakening of Germany's air strength in the East. And the constant reassignment from the Reich to the Eastern front and back again of units which had been numerically weak to begin with consigned the Luftwaffe to a fate of continual attrition and ultimate collapse.

III - The Lack of Strategic Air Warfare against Russia*

Today it is a commonly accepted view among students of military history that the reason for Germany's defeat at the hands of the

---

*"Strategic Air Warfare" is used here to mean warfare waged against an enemy's sources of military strength.

76

Russian giant was the fact that she made no attempt to carry out strategic air warfare.

The first successful blows which resulted in the destruction of those elements of the Soviet air force located in the vicinity of the front were not followed up by systematically planned and accomplished attacks. Nor was any concentrated attempt made to keep Russian armament works and the transportation network under continuous bombardment. The one time this was tried (in 1943), the forces employed were inadequate in number and, due to the critical situation at the front, soon had to be withdrawn. In any case, it was already too late in the game. On the whole, it can be stated that strategic air warfare played no role in Germany's campaign against Soviet Russia.

Why was this the case? To what extent did this sin of omission affect the subsequent course of events?

      *   *   *

There are two things which make it absolutely certain that Luftwaffe leaders intended, from the very beginning, to utilize the newly created air arm in strategic operations in case of war.

In the first place, the Luftwaffe Field Directive on the Conduct of Air Warfare, Section 16,[16] treats strategic air warfare as at least as important as the other two types of aircraft employment. The following is an example:

> Through combat against enemy air forces, the Luftwaffe weakens the enemy's military strength and thereby protects its own military forces, its civilian population, and its country.
>
> Through intervention in operations and combat on the ground and at sea, the Luftwaffe provides direct support for the Army and the Navy.
>
> Through warfare against the sources of enemy military strength and through cutting off communication between these sources and the front, the Luftwaffe seeks to subdue the enemy force.

In Sections 143-178 and 183-185, the Directive goes on to discuss in detail all the various possibilities in strategic air warfare. In

view of the fundamental importance which this Directive was to have as
a basis for operational planning, it is inconceivable that the leaders
of the new service branch could not have been aware of strategic air
warfare as one of their three main missions.

In the second place, we have seen that Luftwaffe leaders devoted
much thought to the development of that type of aircraft which was
indispensible to strategic missions. No less a personage than the
Chief of the Air Command Office, Reichs Air Ministry, (for all practical
purposes, the first Chief of the Luftwaffe General Staff), General
Walther Wever, had openly urged the development of a four-engine bomber.
The fact that this model was known as the "Ural bomber" in Luftwaffe
circles* indicates the intention to wage strategic air warfare in any
future war as well as the probable enemy in any future war.

When we consider the concept of distance implicit in the term
"Ural bomber," we can only conclude that the Luftwaffe top-level command
must have been struck with total blindness when it ordered the project
dropped shortly after Wever's sudden death on 3 June 1936--especially
in view of the fact that both the Dornier and Junkers works had already
built satisfactory test models (the Do-19 and the Ju-89). Shortly
afterwards, the Heinkel works was asked to develop a long-range bomber,
but the resulting model (the He-177)--for reasons we have already dis-
cussed--became buried in a morass of developmental alterations. And
since its development was alternately pushed as rapidly as possible and
completely relegated to the background, depending upon the political
situation and events at the front, the Luftwaffe never had a satisfactory long-range bomber at its disposal, either at the beginning of
the war or during any subsequent phase of it./ It was true that the
first two models, the Do-19 and the Ju-89, while perfectly satisfactory
as far as fuselage design was concerned, had relatively weak engines.
But this problem could certainly have been solved within the three
years remaining before the beginning of the war; and by 1940, or 1941

---

*According to Plocher, Wever invariably called the new model the
"Ural bomber," both in conversation and in internal written communi-
cations with the Reichs Air Ministry. (Plocher, Campaign in the East,
Volume 2, Die Bilanz des Luftwaffeneinsatzes 1941. Erfahrungen und
Erkentnisse aus dem ersten Jahr des Ostfeldzuges (The Balance Sheet
of Luftwaffe Operations for 1941; Experience Gained during the First
Year of the Eastern Campaign), p. 56.

/See above, Chapt. I, Sect. III A and Chapt. 2, Sect. II.

at the latest, the Luftwaffe would have had its long-range, heavily-armored bomber.

Since the four-engine bomber had been scrapped, however, and the He-177 was hopelessly bogged down, the German Luftwaffe had no suitable instrument with which to carry out strategic attacks on the Soviet armaments industry beyond the Urals. Nor did the Luftwaffe possess a suitably powerful long-range fighter. Despite the fact that Goering had expressly instructed Udet to push the development of a fighter capable of ranging over all of England (from bases in Germany!),[17] the Messerschmitt plant, which had long enjoyed a virtual monopoly in the manufacture of fighter aircraft, was never able to produce one.

But it was not the lack of suitable instruments alone which was responsible for the fact that the German Luftwaffe, while piously mouthing Douhet,* began to conduct the ground-support operations of World War II in a manner less modern than that used in World War I,✝ when the BOGOHL's (bomber units of the Army High Command) were effectively utilized in support actions and were even committed in attacks over London.

Shortly after General Wever's death, an energetic young officer of brilliant capabilities, who had already come to General Wever's attention and is supposed to have been selected by him as his prospective successor, began a meteoric rise into the circle of Germany's top-level military leaders. He gradually acquired so much influence that Wever's deputy, General Stumpff, was soon regarded as nothing more than a temporary incumbent in a position which the other was still too young to occupy officially. This new man was Colonel /later Generaloberst/ Hans Jeschonnek. As we have already seen, however, he was an avid champion of the dive-bomber concept as the surest and most economical answer to the problem of bombardment from the air. And it is obvious that the dive-bomber concept of attack could not be realized with a heavy aircraft such as a long-range bomber. Incorrigible until almost the end, Jeschonnek, with his inner aversion to the idea of a four-engine bomber, prevented the development of a long-range bomber. A devotee of tactical warfare from the very beginning, Jeschonnek's own instinctive preferences had been strengthened by his period of service

---

*Editor's Note: Giulio Douhet (1869-1930) Italian general and early exponent of strategic air warfare.

✝This does not apply to the first four campaigns or to the period prior to the Russian campaign.

as commanding officer of the Luftwaffe Training Wing, and by the time he joined the General Staff, he had left the Wever concept of air warfare pretty much behind him.* It is amazing how soon after the death of the first General Staff Chief, the Luftwaffe turned away from the fundamental principles he represented! It is no doubt true that Jeschonnek was strengthened in his insistence on the dive-bomber principle by his inability to imagine that Hitler would become involved in war with an enemy like England. The possibility of a conflict with Russia probably never entered his mind. Since Jeshonnek venerated Hitler as a genius, he understandably felt that it was the Luftwaffe's most noble task to provide the instrument needed to carry out the Fuehrer's plans, i.e. wars against nations such as Czechoslovakia and Poland, which could be and were won in short, sudden campaigns. In his abject inner subordination to Hitler, Jeschonnek was a worthy match for his direct supervisor, Hermann Goering.⌐ It is apparent that these two never gave serious consideration to the ways and means of conducting a remotely possible war against Russia, or in fact against any hypothetical enemy located far away from Germany and having the additional factor of distance on his side.

There was another man, however, perhaps the most energetic personality in the entire Luftwaffe, whose words carried a great deal of weight. This was Colonel /later General and finally Generalfeldmarschall/ Baron von Richthofen. As former commander of the Condor Legion, von Richthofen possessed the advantage of first-hand experience in the testing of German aircraft models in combat against enemy air and land forces. His dive bombers had led the Spanish to ultimate victory over the Communists, and he and Jeschonnek became very close friends. It is very likely that von Richthofen, the Luftwaffe's foremost specialist in close-support operations, did much to strengthen the young General Staff Chief's determination to make direct support of Army operations a decisive factor in achieving a rapid victory on the ground. Von Richthofen was undeniably the dominant personality in the relationship of the two.

The logical result of their thinking was the establishment, shortly before the start of the Polish campaign, of the office of the Special Duty Air Commander and the subsequent commitment of its forces at the main point of action in Poland. It has already been stated that the

------

*Although he certainly would have denied that he was against the concept of strategic air warfare.

⌐See above pp. 11-14.

concept of a specialized air force for missions of this kind was never carried through to its inevitable conclusion.*

The first four campaigns carried out by the German Armed Forces (Poland, Norway, France, and the Balkans) were perfect examples of Hitler's ideal of the short-term, lightning war. In these campaigns the conduct of strategic air operations against the sources of enemy strength proved to be unnecessary, since the theater of operations was of limited extent. In fact, bombardment of the enemy sources of power would have been highly undesirable, since it would have resulted in extensive destruction in areas which Germany wished to exploit to replenish her own strength. These four campaigns placed the resources of Poland (those located in the German sphere of interest), Norway, the occupied area of France, and the occupied portions of the Balkan countries and Greece at Germany's disposal. Thus, all of these resources were then available to the German military economy and to German transport requirements./

Despite the experience gathered during the Battle of Britain in regard to aircraft range, Germany did not take advantage of its year of preparation for the Russian conflict to alter the organization of Luftwaffe units/ or to make any changes in the contemplated methods of their employment. The members of the Luftwaffe top-level command apparently were not gifted with sufficient imagination to visualize clearly the potential requirements of a war against Russia, with its enormous geographic extent and, consequently, its sharply varying climatic conditions. They were going by established traditions, and the exigencies of administration left no room for new, creative thinking. In addition, of course, we cannot ignore the possibility that the young General Staff Chief, blinded by his veneration for Hitler and his unreasoning faith in the latter's genius, may really have believed in Hitler's assurances that the campaign in Russia would also turn out to be a short-term operation.

Taken literally, however, established tradition called for a sudden

---

*See above, Chapt. 2, Sect. II.

/The German bombardment of the Potez works in the vicinity of Paris on 3 June 1940, just a few days before the capture of Paris, was completely wrong from the point of view of efficient strategic air warfare.

/See Plocher, Campaign in the East, and above, Chapt. 2, Sect. II.

surprise attack on the enemy's air forces, in order to paralyze them into inactivity, and an immediate follow-up in the form of direct and indirect air support of ground operations, in order to assure a quick victory for the Army.

In view of the confidence which the Luftwaffe was still able to inspire in Hitler as late as 1941, it can be assumed with a fair degree of certainty that Luftwaffe leaders were consulted in detail prior to the issuance of Fuehrer Directive 21, dated 18 December 1940. Therefore, we have every right to assume that the views expressed therein in regard to the employment of air forces* are in accordance with the opinions and intentions of the Luftwaffe's top-level command.

The order to attack (BARBAROSSA), dated 18 December 1940, made the prior attainment of certain ground victories a prerequisite of strategic

---

*In Fuehrer Directive No. 21, under "Conduct of Operations, B. Luftwaffe," the following appears:

> It will be the responsibility of the Luftwaffe to neutralize the effectiveness of the Russian air forces as rapidly as possible and to destroy them as soon as is practicable. In addition, the Luftwaffe will provide direct support for the Army at those points where it is most needed, i.e. for the Army Group Center and for the southern flank of the Army Group South. In order of their significance for enemy operations, Russian railway lines will be paralyzed and the most important, obvious objectives, (such as river crossings) taken by means of daring action by parachute and airlanding forces. In order to concentrate the entire striking power upon the enemy air force and on direct support of the Army, the armament industry is not to be attacked during the course of the main operations. Not until the mobile war has been brought under control will such projects be undertaken, and then they will be directed chiefly against the Ural region.

(Der Fuehrer and Oberste Befehlshaber der Wehrmacht OKW/WFSt/Abt.L (I) No. 33408/40 g. K. Chefs. 18.12.1940, Weisung No. 21. Fall Barbarossa (The Fuehrer and Supreme Commander, Armed Forces, Armed Forces High Command/Armed Forces Operations Staff/Branch Luftwaffe (I), No. 33408/40, Classified, dated 18 December 1940, Directive No. 21, Barbarossa), copy in G/a, Karlsruhe Document Collection.)

air operations. And then, the Luftwaffe would be utilized only in order to hold enemy potential down to a minimum, after the ground campaign had already been won. The BARBAROSSA order, incidentally, spoke only of a "short campaign."

During the period 22-30 June, the blows which the German Luftwaffe directed against the enemy airfields lying within her reach were completely successful. The Russians allegedly suffered materiel losses amounting to 4,990 aircraft of all types; as a result, the Russian air forces were incapacitated for a number of weeks, at least in the areas assigned to the Army Groups North and Center. In these sectors, then, the Luftwaffe had achieved air supremacy; in the sector assigned to the Army Group South, it had air superiority.[18]

Considering the significance of this situation, together with the fact that the Soviet fighter forces were extremely cautious during the period immediately following, we are justified in concluding (without being accused of wishful thinking) that the attacks carried out by the Luftwaffe on those Russian aircraft works (or rather armament works in general) lying within its range were highly successful. At that time the Russians did not yet have the strong antiaircraft artillery with which they were later able to protect their industrial plants, power works, and railway stations.

On the whole, however, the Luftwaffe struck against the Russian air force rather than against the Russian aircraft industry. True, the Russians did sustain considerable aircraft losses thereby; however, the crews were not permanently put out of action. And the Russians were usually successful in managing to remove their aircraft plants (machines and other equipment) from those areas threatened by the German advance into regions where German air attack was out of the question because they lay beyond the range of the German bombers. Production was soon resumed in the new locations, and with it the first step was taken in the establishment of a strong Russian air arm; by the end of the war, its strength--at least in terms of numbers--was significant. This recovery would never have been possible if Germany had been able to accompany her attack on the Russian airfields (carried out by light and medium bombers) with a surprise attack with four-engine bombers against the Russian aircraft plants located near the front, particularly those in Moscow and Voronezh. The fairly desperate situation of the Russian air units assigned to the front must have been an indication of a similar situation in Russian industry. Even the American deliveries, which also would have been more vulnerable to attack by four-engine rather than by twin-engine bombers, would probably not have been able to help the Russians out of their difficulties.

And to think how many other rewarding enemy targets there were, some of them entirely unprotected--the Russian tank works, power stations, oil refineries, transport networks, and communication lines!

As we have seen, however, the four-engine bomber had been dropped in 1937 and the long-range He-177 was nowhere near ready for employment at the front. In short, Germany did not possess the one weapon which would have had the range, bomb-carrying capacity, and armament strength needed in the present instance. Nevertheless, Germany's medium bombers could also have inflicted serious damage on Russian armament works, power plants, and traffic centers lying quite far behind the front lines, especially if such bombardment had been carried out at the beginning of hostilities.*

There are two commonly used excuses for why this was not done, and neither of them is valid. The first of these excuses states that it would not have been possible to combine extensive air support of Army ground operations with the conduct of strategic air warfare. As we have repeatedly pointed out, Hitler's demand for direct air support of the Army in the East clearly implied that at least one tactical air command should be available for each Army group. The activation of these tactical commands, in turn, demanded that Germany's aircraft production (this time, single-engine aircraft) finally be brought up to a level commensurate with an all-out armament effort, in other words, that it be increased much more than was actually the case during the first months of the war and even throughout 1940 and 1941. According to the plans for BARBAROSSA, four air corps were to be employed in Russia. Once the production of single-engine aircraft had been increased to the necessary level, the twin-engine aircraft (twenty-eight groups in all) could have been withdrawn and placed under a unified bomber command for commitment in strategic air operations. Even if a part of these twenty-eight groups had been deviated to indirect support actions for the ground forces, the remainder would still have been sufficient for strategic warfare requirements. And a clear separation of tactical and strategic air units, which would have been achieved by the reassignment of the twin-engine bombers, would have done much to clarify the problem of organization and that of the validity of existing concepts regarding the conduct of air warfare. The strategic units would have been freed of the necessity of providing direct support (as opposed to "indirect" support) for the Army, a mission which they were simply not equipped to fulfill; and at last there would have been sufficient units available

---

*That is, immediately after the Russian air forces had been subdued, which happened during the first few days of action.

84

which were specifically suited to air operations in the sense advocated by Douhet.

The second excuse given is that the Luftwaffe Field Directive No. 16 required the commitment of all Luftwaffe strength* during the decisive battle. This is as invalid as the first excuse. Such commitment was rather to be spread over the entire campaign, beginning with the first day of operations and continuing until the campaign had been brought to a successful conclusion, presumably within three months. It is obvious that the Army would have received the all-out Luftwaffe support required by the BARBAROSSA directive despite the simultaneous launching of strategic air warfare, if armament planning and the training program had been carried out as has been suggested above. On the whole, the degree of support furnished the Army would have been even greater. We might also point out that a campaign of the contemplated duration (three months) could hardly be termed a decisive battle within the meaning of Directive No. 16. If the enemy's industrial plants were permitted to work on undistrubed during this period, they would provide, as indeed they actually did, a continual stream of materiel reinforcements for the Soviet Army at the front throughout the duration of the "decisive battle." This continuing reinforcement played a significant role in helping the Russian armies to hold out in one of the most decisive campaigns in the history of Russia.

*   *   *

A large Luftwaffe bomber command could and should have been set up! It goes without saying that a part of this large force could have been utilized to provide effective indirect support for the ground forces at points where it might be required.

This force of twenty-eight groups of medium bombers could also have been augmented by the 4th and 27th Bomber Groups, which the Commander in Chief, Luftwaffe, had been forced to retain in the West until the summer of 1941. They would have had excellent operating conditions in the East, especially after early August, when the German forces reached Smolensk. For a time at least, the Commander in Chief, Luftwaffe, would have had a force of thirty-four medium bomber groups at his disposal. Together with single-engine fighters, reconnaissance aircraft, and other special duty machines, there would have been nearly nine full wings, easily enough to form an additional air fleet.

----

*This, of course, would include all twin-engine aircraft.

85

We can hardly imagine what the commitment of a force of this size might have meant in 1941, when Russian antiaircraft artillery was not nearly so effective as it was in 1944, when the IV Air Corps carried out its attacks with frequent success. Each Russian tank, each gun, each airplane, each railway locomotive which could be destroyed while still in the factory saved the German Army serious losses.

The importance of this statement becomes clear when we consider that Soviet Russia, according to estimates made by Eike Middeldorf, produced a total of approximately 150,000 tanks during World War II. And while Russia could commit her entire tank production against Germany and Germany's weak allies (i.e. on a single front), Germany had to spread her production of approximately 25,000 tanks[19] over Russia, the Mediterranean, the Balkans, and--later--the invasion front, not to mention the quota which went to her allies. German destruction of enemy tanks on the Eastern front was purchased at the cost of tremendous effort--by sacrificial commitment of German infantry, far too ill-equipped with armor-piercing weapons; or by the employment, invariably accompanied by heavy losses, of the Luftwaffe. In connection with the latter, the remarkable record achieved by Colonel Rudel deserves special mention--510 kills! In contrast, a single successful air attack on the Russian tank factories would have destroyed the product of several weeks' work all at once and would have been sufficient to stop any further production for some time. It is difficult to stop a rushing stream; its source, however, can be dammed up with relatively little effort.

The fact that the BARBAROSSA Directive did not specifically require strategic air warfare along with direct air support of the ground forces* was, admittedly, a serious error on the part of command, and the Army High Command cannot be absolved of at least a portion of the blame for it. If Germany's military leaders had recognized in time the need for a reorganization of Luftwaffe forces and a revitalization of the air armament program, the necessary resources would have been at hand when the need for additional activations became apparent.

It is completely beyond understanding, however, that the Luftwaffe General Staff Chief made no attempt to salvage the situation later on, for it must have been obvious by November 1941 at the latest that the war with Russia could not be concluded in a short campaign but was

---

*Although, as pointed out in Chapt. 2, Sect. II, a separate bomber command could not be established until the close-support forces could be strengthened by a substantial increase in the production of single-engine aircraft.

turning into a long-term struggle whose ultimate duration could not be foreseen. With practically no interfence from Germany, Russia had been able to move her armament works out of the path of the German advance to safer locations far to the East. The few strategic attacks carried out by the Luftwaffe in 1941 were isolated incidents.*

In Plocher's opinion,[20] the proper course of action in October/November 1941 (when it must have been apparent that the blitzkrieg was doomed to failure) would have been for the Luftwaffe and Army General Staffs to submit a joint recommendation to the Commander in Chief, Wehrmacht, suggesting that operations be interrupted for the moment in order to prepare for an all-out strategic air offensive. During the winter of 1941/42, Plocher continues, a clear organizational delineation between strategic and tactical Luftwaffe units could have been effected, together with a clarification of the command channels involved.[21]

From today's vantage point, the winter of 1941/42 seems to be a very late date for such basic alterations. Still it represented the last possible opportunity to prepare thoroughly for a decisive strategic air offensive.

We cannot pretend, of course, that the general situation at this time was particularly favorable for fundamental organizational changes. The Luftwaffe was bogged down in the midst of direct ground-support actions for the German Army, hindered by the fact of its own state of near-exhaustion, by the ruthlessness of the continual Russian attacks, and by the Russian winter. Any attempt to withdraw the bomber forces (i.e. those which had not been withdrawn already to replace losses in other units) would have invited the danger of serious setbacks at the front. Moreover, the Technical Office was in the middle of a difficult period of reorganization--as a result of Udet's suicide on 17 November 1941 and the subsequent assumption of his duties by Milch, as the new Chief of Procurement and Supply--and found itself confronted by the difficult assignment of replacing the heavy losses occasioned by the advent of the Russian winter, the surprising success achieved by the

---

*The only target which was bombarded systematically was Moscow, which was heavily protected by antiaircraft artillery, searchlights, and night fighter aircraft. During the period 21/22 July 1941 through 5 April 1942, the Luftwaffe carried out a total of seventy-six daytime attacks and eleven night raids against Moscow. (Plocher, Campaign in the East, Appendix Volume for 1941, Appendix 60. Plocher credits his data to General von Rhoden, without indicating any specific source.)

enemy's continuing attacks, and the first retreat operations of the German Army. There is no denying that the muddy period, with its relative slacking-off of military operations, would have been more suitable for a reorganization of strategic and tactical Luftwaffe forces.

Reorganization, then, and the new activations which it entailed, represented difficult problems. Its concomitant result, however, (increased production in dive bombers, close-support aircraft, and fighters) would have provided Germany's air armament industry with a tangible goal and would certainly have served as a spur to Milch's ambition and energy. We can assume with a fair degree of certainty that the production goal could have been met at that time, despite the general military situation, without the necessity of Hitler's assigning the Luftwaffe a new priority rating for the allocation of raw materials. The Luftwaffe could have been ready to conduct strategic air warfare against Soviet targets by the fall of 1942. And the effects of strategic warfare would have made themselves felt in a very short time. For one thing, a good deal of Russian antiaircraft artillery would have been tied down far behind the lines and would thus have been kept from commitment at the front. The Luftwaffe close-support forces would have continued to provide even more direct and indirect support for the ground forces, while the long-range bomber wings could have gone on to attack the Russian armaments works and other sources of military strength. The spring of 1943 would have marked the climax of the effectiveness of strategic air operations, and in the meantime the German Army at least would have reaped a number of benefits.

*   *   *

Colonel Fritz Kless, first operations officer and later general staff chief of the Air Command Center (later to become the Sixth Air Fleet), was untiring in his efforts to persuade Luftwaffe leaders of the need for strategic air operations,[22] until finally the Luftwaffe High Command agreed to permit the employment of bomber aircraft against the Russian rubber plant at Yaroslavl and the tank factory at Gorki, an indication of the fact that Jeschonnek had allowed himself to be persuaded shortly before his death. The organization of Luftwaffe forces suitable for strategic air operations into the IV Air Corps was not confirmed until 26 November 1943, in a Directive issued by the Commander in Chief, Luftwaffe.[23] The following is quoted from this Directive:

> In order to carry out systematic bombardment of
> Russian armament industries, I intend to unite the
> majority of the heavy bomber units assigned in the
> East--together with other special duty bomber units--
> under the command of the Headquarters, IV Air Corps.

88

These units will be assigned the mission of conducting air attacks against the Russian armaments industry with a view to destroying Soviet materiel resources--tanks, artillery, and aircraft--before they can be put to use at the front. In this way, the Luftwaffe will be able to provide greater relief for our hard-pressed Eastern armies than by its commitment in ground-support operations alone.

Understandably, no one wanted to admit that this action was being taken far too late to be of any real help. In the meantime, in a study dated 9 November 1943,[24] the Luftwaffe Operations Staff had prepared a fairly realistic appraisal of the situation. Under Point 1, the following statement is made: "Up to and including the attainment of the Dnieper line in the fall of 1941, the German Luftwaffe was properly employed in the Eastern campaign. The defeat of the Soviet air forces and the providing of direct support in ground operations made a rapid advance possible." From that point on, the study continues, at least a portion of Luftwaffe strength should have been diverted to operations against the Russian railway lines far behind the front, in order to prevent the evacuation of enemy industry to the rear area, and against those factories still operating within bomber range of the front. The study goes on to say that operations of this sort, as well as the effective bombardment of Moscow and Leningrad, were rendered impossible by the need for continuing close-support actions for the ground forces. As a result, large-scale attacks on enemy industry could be carried out only sporadically (on Voronezh, Stalingrad, Saratov, and Grozny, for example, during the summer of 1943)--although with great success. As the study indicates, the recovery of the Soviet air forces (as a matter of fact, their achievement of numerical superiority) and <u>the disappearance of the most rewarding industrial targets from Luftwaffe bomber range</u>,* as a result of the German retreat, soon altered the situation. Point 4 of the study continues: "We have no choice but to admit that we let the most favorable moment slip through our hands; in the meantime the difficulties have become very great. Moreover, our Luftwaffe forces are now tied down more than ever in the East."

This was a bitter admission to make. The Luftwaffe Operations Staff still hoped to be able to "demolish at least the largest Russian armament works in the Moscow-Upper Volga industrial area" with "a relatively small force," a project which was to be given top priority and which would be

---

*Underlining by the author of this study.

executed through the employment of new aircraft types (He-177, Ju-290, etc.) which would have to be forthcoming "soon and in adequate numbers."

During the spring of 1944, the IV Air Corps* carried out a series of attacks with what, in the words of some of the participants, was "very good success."[25] Soon after the Russian breakthrough on the front sector assigned to the Army Group Center (on 18 June 1944), these attacks had to be discontinued, the 4th Bomber Wing flying its last bombardment mission during the night of 22/23 July 1944.[26]

Strategic air warfare,/ begun far too late, had to be broken off because the Eastern armies, threatened with decimation, were beginning to scream for help, and the bombers were assigned to direct ground-support operations.

That was the end. All later plans for strategic air operations in the East--born of a hopelessly unrealistic optimism--were doomed to frustration.

IV - Malta - the Victory Germany Gave Away

During the second half of May 1941, the German Armed Forces--General Student's/ paratroopers and the 6th Mountain Division--had seized the island of Crete. The extremely heavy losses suffered during the first few days of this daring action frightened both Hitler and Goering into dropping their original plan of occupying Cyprus immediately afterwards. If this plan had been realized, the balance of power in the eastern Mediterranean would have been weighted in favor of the Axis.

The possession of Crete alone proved to be fairly insignificant in the long run. Malta, on the other hand, a much tinier island than Crete,

---

*The following bomber forces were assigned to the IV Air Corps: 3d Bomber Wing (I and II Group), 4th Bomber Wing (II and III Group), 55th Bomber Wing (I, II, and III Group, but without the ice-squadron /so called because equipped to land on ice/), 100th Bomber Wing (III Group).

/Insofar as we can speak of strategic air warfare here, since the majority of the missions flown were against railway targets.

/Editor's Note: Generaloberst Kurt Student, best known for his direction of the German paratroop and airlanding operations in Holland (10-14 May 1940), for his planning of the German glider attack on the Belgian Fort Eben-Emael (11 May 1940), and for his role in the seizure of Crete (20 May-1 June 1941).

was one of Britain's most vital bases at that time, despite its remote and isolated position. Possession of Malta decided the fate of shipping from Italy and North Africa and thus the efficacy of the supply line to Rommel's armies. For the British it was also an invaluable intermediate base between Gibraltar and Alexandria, with stockpiles of coal and oil, well-equipped wharves and docks, and--above all--with its location right in the middle of the Mediterranean. Moreover, the island had high morale value as a symbol of British sea power. The scene of some of the proudest moments of British naval history, Malta was a measure of England's mastery of the Mediterranean.

The island is located fifty-six miles south of the eastern coast of Sicily and is approximately 225 miles distant from the African coast at Tunis. Its area is only 153 square miles, and the loftiest peak is no more than 846 feet. The width of the island varies between six and seven and one-half miles. Its population, military and civilian, was about 300,000 during the war. The British had an armed force of approximately 30,000 men on Malta, including the militia made up of Maltese volunteers and the armed labor troops. Its nucleus was the 231st Malta Brigade Group, which, in 1941, consisted of three British battalions (2d Battalion, Devonshire Regiment; 1st Battalion, Hampshire Regiment; and 1st Battalion, Dorsetshire Regiment). Its mission was to guard the Maltese coastline of twenty-eight miles, nineteen of which--according to British data--were highly suitable for the landing of an armed force.[27]

Italy neglected to capture the island right after her entry into the war, presumably because she had no wish to test her strength in an inevitable encounter with Britain's Mediterranean fleet. The consequences of her neglect, however, became more and more painfully evident as the conflict in North Africa approached its climax. They became apparent to Germany when she came to the aid of the Italians in 1941, after the latter had already been defeated by British forces and were in danger of losing all of Tripolitania. The later difficulties of the Africa Corps could be attributed almost exclusively to the unreliability of the supply line across the Mediterranean. At various times, fairly large British fleet units were stationed at Malta and, using the island as a base of operations, submarines and bombers were able to attack German shipping convoys--usually not very well protected by their alleged escort of Italian warships--and inflict serious damage. In September 1941, the damage amounted to $38\frac{1}{2}\%$ of the total tonnage shipped; in October the figure was 63%, and in November it hit a peak of 77%.[28]

Urgently as every single aircraft was needed to assure the rapid success of the Russian campaign in 1941, Hitler, in October of that year, had no alternative but to send the Second Air Fleet to Sicily (where he had already transferred the X Air Corps from Norway in December 1940). He did this to protect shipping activity and to eliminate or at least neutralize Malta, that most dangerous "aircraft carrier." Apparently the Second Air Fleet's presence in Sicily and the force of its first attacks must have had a very salutary effect, for during January 1942 only 20% of the total tonnage was lost through enemy action, and Rommel had a chance to catch his breath.

It is understandable that Germany's naval leaders submitted their recommendations for the conquest of Malta to Hitler at a very early date, even before the occupation of Crete. Generaloberst a. D. Student, reports on a conference with Hitler on 21 April 1941 to discuss plans for the Crete operation. Keitel and Jodl unexpectedly raised the question of whether it might not be wiser for the overall course of operations in the Mediterranean to take Malta first and let Crete wait until afterwards. With the reply, "Malta will be taken care of later!", Hitler decided on Crete.[29]

The first member of the Luftwaffe to broach the subject of Malta to Hitler was Feldmarschall Kesselring, who insisted that occupation of the island was absolutely indispensible to efficient conduct of the war in Africa. Kesselring reports that he was unable to get Hitler's approval for this project until the spring of 1942, at which time Hitler put an end to Kesselring's impassioned oratory by patting him on the arm and saying, "Just take it easy, Feldmarschall Kesselring; I'll do it all right!"[30]

In Italian military circles, Marshal Cavallero was the officer most convinced of the necessity for taking the island. He established a special Malta staff under the command of General Gaudin.

In February 1942, Germany began making careful preparations for large-scale air operations against Malta.* The attacks began on 2 April 1942 and continued throughout the whole month; according to Boehmler,[31] the last full-scale raid was carried out on 10 May. During April and May, the Luftwaffe flew 11,000 sorties against Malta;[32] approximately one-fourth of the bomb load dropped was directed at the antiaircraft artillery positions on the island. By the end of May, there were no more submarines or warships at the island. All the enemy aircraft based there had been destroyed, and the antiaircraft batteries, forty of which

---

*Even before this time, small air raids had been carried out untiringly.

were concentrated around La Valetta, fired only sporadically. Both troops and civilian population were already feeling the pinch of rapidly diminishing supply stocks, and resistance could be considered very weak. "Even so, the Luftwaffe had not succeeded in destroying the island's defending forces, since the huge subterranean limestone caves afforded them sufficient protection."[33]

After this initial success, which unfortunately could not be followed up immediately by a landing of German and Italian troops, came the usual tragedy--the advent of war on several fronts. Kesselring writes as follows:[34]

> With the success of the Luftwaffe raids on Malta, the Armed Forces High Command considered the situation to be so well under control that it transferred the majority of the Luftwaffe forces to the East. Naturally, enough units remained in the Mediterranean to keep Malta under surveillance, to harass enemy convoys, and to protect our own convoys--without having to draw upon the units assigned to the Air Commander Africa. In the long run, however, these units were too weak to prevent the recovery of Malta and to keep supplies from reaching the island fortress indefinitely.

In the meantime, the two allies concluded their negotiations for the joint offensive, after the Armed Forces High Command had announced Germany's willingness to participate on 21 April. Mussolini arrived at Hitler's headquarters on Obersalzberg on 29 April, and he was soon followed by Marshal Cavallero and Count Ciano. Their meeting had been called to decide on the date of the attack. Cavallero wanted it to take place before Rommel began his offensive. Kesselring, who originally had been of the same opinion, now insisted that Rommel would have to defeat the British first.[35] When the conference ended on 30 April 1942, it had been decided that Rommel's attack, slated for the end of May, should come first. As soon as his initial advance was successfully completed, Rommel was to remain at the Halfaya Pass on the Egyptian border, and the Malta operation would be carried out. The attack on the island, christened Operation HERCULES, was to take place no later than the full-moon period in July.[36]

So much for the agreements reached by the heads of state and their military advisors. Behind the scenes, the picture was quite different.

Ciano, who always regarded events with a good deal of skepticism, noted the following in his diary under date of 28 April: ". . . whether the undertaking will ever take place and, if so, when, is quite another matter . . . ." On 31 May, after an interview with General Carboni, who was to be in command of the attacking divisions, he writes "He is dead set against it (the operation). He is convinced that we'll suffer very high losses and that we won't accomplish anything at all. He blames Cavallero for everything and seems to think that he is an intriguer and not to be trusted."[37]

Far more important, however, were Hitler's feelings in the matter. The losses sustained by the Luftwaffe during the occupation of Crete had made him very skeptical about paratrooper operations, and besides he was not at all certain that Malta was ripe for attack. Then, too, if the island were captured, the necessity of maintaining it would arise--still another area to eat up Germany's resources.

Rommel, in the meantime, who had launched his offensive on 26 May 1942, had succeeded, after heavy fighting against the British forces around Bir Hakim, in gaining a clear victory and had taken Tobruk by storm (on 20 June). In accordance with the agreement reached, Rommel should have brought his operations to a halt and certain air units assigned to the Air Commander Africa should have been released for commitment in Operation HERCULES.*

The conference of marshals on 26 June at Sidi el Barani, Rommel's headquarters, attended by Kesselring and Rommel (for the German side) and Bastico and Cavallero (for the Italian), showed very clearly the discrepancy between Kesselring's and Rommel's views. Kesselring's warning that it was dangerous to advance against the enemy air bases on the Nile (manned by fully prepared fresh forces) with nearly exhausted Luftwaffe units which urgently needed time to rest and recover, was impatiently brushed aside by Rommel. When Bastico asked for his appraisal of the situation, Rommel gave his word that he could be in Cairo within ten days. Under these circumstances, Bastico and Cavallero, heretofore against immediate continuation of operations in Africa, gave in. The other dissenter, Kesselring, was ordered to stop objecting in a radiogram from Hitler.[38]

---

*As a matter of fact, this reassignment was already in process, which made it difficult to continue the pursuit of the retreating British troops. (Luftlage in Afrika (The Air Situation in Africa), an extract of a postwar study prepared by a number of German officers, p. 12; G/VII/10a, Karlsruhe Document Collection.)

94

Hitler, to whom Rommel had direct access through Ministry Director
Dr. J. W. Berndt--assigned to Rommel's staff as an aide--, wrote to
Mussolini in order to obtain his approval for the immediate continuation
of Rommel's operations and the postponement of Operation HERCULES. General von Rintelen, military attache in Rome, gave Il Duce Hitler's
famous letter, which contained a reference to the fact that "no man can
wear the laurels of victory more than once." Von Rintelen reports that
Il Duce "looked at me arrogantly and was extremely enthusiastic at the
prospect of an immediate offensive against Egypt in order to capture
the cities of Cairo and Alexandria. At this stage of operations, Mussolini still had unlimited confidence in Hitler's military genius. Cavallero and his objections were simply brushed aside . . . . he had no
alternative but to alter his orders and to postpone the Malta undertaking
until September."39

While von Rintelen's report would seem to indicate that Rommel
attained approval for the postponement of Operation HERCULES, Generaloberst Student's report of his conversation with Hitler in early June
(prior to Rommel's victory at Bir Hakim) contradicts this interpretation
completely. Student, according to his report, submitted to Hitler his
plan for the conquest of Malta; the latter, after listening patiently
to his explanations, agreed with him that the establishment of a bridgehead would be possible. He continued, however:

> I can assure you, though, that as soon as we
> begin our attack, the Gibraltar squadrons will
> take to the air and the British fleet will set
> sail from Alexandria. You can imagine how the
> Italians will react to that. The minute they
> get the news on their radios, they'll all make
> a dash for the harbors of Sicily--both warships
> and freighters. You'll be sitting all alone
> on the island with your paratroopers.

According to Student's report, he was unable to change Hitler's
mind. Hitler decided that the attack on Malta should be postponed until
after 1942, and Student was not even permitted to return to Italy. He
merely reported to Kesselring by telephone; the latter was extremely
upset.40 Is it possible that Student might have been mistaken in the
date? It seems very strange that Kesselring knew nothing about it!

According to a report prepared by General Koller, the last General
Staff Chief, Goering accepted the credit for having persuaded the Fuehrer
to drop the plans for the occupation of Malta. "Unfortunately, the
motivating factor was his fear of losing his paratrooper forces."41

This attitude on Goering's part is confirmed by Feldmarschall Kesselring's personal experiences during this period and can be accepted as an established fact.*

Malta, then, although it was near to surrender in April 1942,/ was

---

*Kesselring's own words are:

> In Goering, Hitler had a loyal supporter for his own aversion to an attack on Malta. Goering was afraid of another Crete, with its "huge" losses, although in reality the two operations had nothing whatsoever in common. Hitler was delighted when Rommel's victory at Tobruk enabled him to call off the Malta operation without losing face. I explained to Goering again and again that, after the Luftwaffe raids of April and May, Malta could be taken with a minimum of loss; the longer we waited, the greater and more costly the effort to be made. The Italian Commando Supremo was being beset with ever more adamant objections on the part of naval leaders. Failure to carry out Operation HERCULES would seriously jeopardize the success of overall operations in the Mediterranean. (Kesselring, p. 169.)

In this connection, see also Goering's remark of 1 June 1945, "Just try to carry out a joint invasion with the Italians!" (Vernehmung von Hermann Goering, 1 June 1945 (Interrogation of Hermann Goering, 1 June 1945), p. 45, D/I/2, Karlsruhe Document Collection.)

/How close Malta was to surrender can be ascertained from Gilchrist's remarks:

> Perhaps the most difficult thing to bear was the general feeling that Malta's existence could be compared with that of a prisoner sentenced to death with no hope of reprieve. The hardest fight for most of us was not that against the enemy attackers, but against an all-pervading feeling of depression. Some of the men were able to remain optimistic because of their faith in the "boat" myth. Although it seemed highly unlikely to those in the know, these men persisted in their belief that, when the situation became really serious, a boat would come to take them back home. Those of us who thought realistically could take no comfort in this belief . . . . (Gilchrist, p. 11.)

never taken; it remained an extremely sharp thorn in the side of Germany's conduct of war in the Mediterranean and helped immensely to make final victory possible for the Anglo-American task forces. What preparations were actually made for Operation HERCULES? According to information provided by Generaloberst a. D. Student, who had been placed in charge of the airlanding operation, the plan was to begin with a paratrooper landing along the southwestern coast of the island. This phase of the action was to be carried out by Student's own XI Air Corps, together with the Italian Parachute Division "Folgore," which General Ramcke had trained "in record time and very effectively." The airlanding force was to be brought to the island by freight gliders, of which 1,000 were available for the operation. The southwestern coast--which had never been fortified because of its inaccessability--and one small fishing port there, could also be used for the landing of tanks if this should prove necessary. It was unfortunate that reconnaissance of the coast, to be accomplished by divers from the Italian Navy Regiment "San Marco," was subject to innumerable delays.[42]

Once a bridgehead had been formed, the Axis forces would be right in front of the Victoria Line, a row of fortified positions running across the island from east to west. In their breakthrough of the Victoria Line, the paratrooper and airlanding forces were to be reinforced by several Italian divisions landed by boat. The result would be an overwhelmingly large attack force combined with perfect air cover. Although British resistance on Malta would certainly be stubborn, all in all conditions could be regarded as far more favorable than they had been on Crete. The second wave of transport aircraft could reach Malta much more quickly and, because of the relatively short distance between the island and the base of operations in Sicily, four or five missions could be flown daily.[43]

It could be safely assumed that British fleet units would not appear before the end of the first day of operations. Britain had too few aircraft carriers, and besides they would have represented far too vulnerable a target for the Luftwaffe forces around the island. In case of emergency, the Axis transport ships could always alter course to remain within running distance of Pantelleria or Tripoli. If British bombers were employed from bases in Africa, they would have to fly without escort and would be easy game for the German fighters.[44]

It is Generaloberst Student's firm belief that German military leaders had every reason to count on the airlanding's being a success. The II Air Corps, the Second Air Fleet--with Feldmarschall Kesselring as guiding spirit of the plan--, and even Hitler himself were all of this opinion. Nor could there be any doubt as to the outcome of the landing of the forces transported by sea; the transport ships would be escorted by Italian warships and the long spring day would afford ideal conditions for providing effective air cover. Even without this landing, however, Student's original force--constantly reinforced from the air--would probably be sufficient.

But what was to happen next? The enemy had two alternatives; either he could defend the Victoria Line or he could attempt to push the landing force back into the sea. At that time there was no reliable information available as to his fire power. One thing was definite, however; no matter which course of action he selected, he would be forced to make his troops mobile, to occupy his firing positions, and to set up a system of supply lines. And, so far as it was possible to tell, he had no more antiaircraft artillery available to cover these operations. It was reasonably certain that all the antiaircraft artillery on the island had already been brought into action in order to protect the harbor of La Valetta and other important military and industrial installations against the German air attacks. If a part of this artillery (which had already been seriously weakened by German air attack) were diverted to cover the operations of the troops fighting in the interior and to combat German aircraft and tanks, then it would be too widely dispersed to be effective anywhere, and the entire island would be defenseless against the destruction wrought by German bombardment. In the last analysis, then, it would have been the enemy's own defensive operations which hastened the downfall of the island.

It is certain that Hitler's aversion to the operation, like Goering's was influenced by the fear that it could result in paratroop losses as high as those suffered in the Crete operation. The airlanding on Crete, however, had been followed by a mishap which Germany had learned to avoid in the meantime. Besides, Crete was much farther away from Athens than the target area in Malta was from the contemplated base of operations. In Crete, the landing force had operated at three widely-separated points of attack; in Malta there was only one, and the ultimate goal, La Valetta, was only about six miles away from the initial landing area. In the case of Malta, the Luftwaffe could even have established an airlift if it had been necessary.

The considerations detailed above would have retained their validity even if the Italian fleet had failed to intervene (though this was not very likely, since Hitler had made it clear to his Italian ally that the Armed Forces High Command intended to carry out Operation HERCULES, either alone or jointly with Italy). Italy, in her reluctance to leave Malta entirely to Germany, would certainly have hastened the training of the San Marco and Folgore divisions.

The difficulty was that Hitler simply could not accept the necessity for the Malta operation. He could not bring himself to recognize its urgency. He let Italy take the initiative, despite the fact that it was German soldiers--not Italian--who were going to their death on the way to Africa because the British were sinking the troop transports-- all too often left to fend for themselves by their Italian escort ships--with warships and aircraft based at Malta. Even if Hitler refused to entertain the thought of carrying out Operation HERCULES without his Italian ally (because of his almost pathological loyalty to Mussolini), still he was skeptical enough of Italy's dependability and sense of duty that he was not quite willing to insist on Italian assistance at any price.

The Luftwaffe bombardment of Malta, in the end, was in vain. The fruit was ripe, but it was never plucked. The island, which regarded its escape as a miracle, soon managed to recover its equilibrium. And as soon as it facilities had been restored to the point where British aircraft could land and British ships could utilize its harbors, the thorn in the Axis side began to throb again. Then, in the fall of the same year, the reversals suffered by Rommel at El Alamein and the Allied landing at Casablanca brought Germany and Italy into a situation they could no longer master. And as the fighting in Tunisia progressed, Malta's importance increased tremendously. Again, it was the Luftwaffe which had to pay the price for Goering's senseless interference. Heavy losses and rapid attrition of materiel (in Naples-based operations to provide cover for the transport convoys), especially of the Ju-52 aircraft employed in air supply operations to Tunisia, were the results. If Malta had been taken in 1942, it is probable that Rommel would not have suffered defeat, and that the Allied landing in North Africa--if tried at all--would have come to an inconclusive end in the mountains of Algeria. Last, but definitely not least, civilian morale in the Axis nations would have been greatly bolstered!

As it was, however, Tunisia capitulated, Sicily was lost, Il Duce was deposed, and Italy withdrew from the war; Naples was lost--and with it the airfields at Foggia--, then Rome, and finally, in April 1945, came the collapse of Germany's operations in the Italian theater of war. One catastrophe after another!

Victory in Malta--a foregone conclusion--would have certainly prevented this catastrophe; but Germany allowed this victory to slip through her fingers.

V - Stalingrad.

The history of operations at Stalingrad will always remain a psychological and military riddle.

Adolph Hitler, the Fuehrer and Supreme Commander of the Armed Forces, had long viewed with uneasiness the developments taking place along the bend of the Don River,[45] where Rumanian and Italian troops were stationed--troops which were no match for the Russians as regarded strength, defensive power, and equipment. A German reserve force (the 22d Armored Division), which was simply assumed without further ado to be sufficiently large and well-equipped, was not dispatched to the threatened area until the last minute. It was not yet fully prepared for action on 19 November 1942, when the Russians broke through the Axis lines at Serafymovich and Kletskaya.

In addition, since the end of August 1942, fighting had been going on for the possession of Stalingrad, where the German Sixth Army was involved in a difficult frontal attack against a large city which became all the more impenetrable as its factories and apartment houses were turned into ruins that provided ideal cover for the defenders. The Germans were unable to control the Volga, and the Russians continued to bring supplies and reinforcements to their hard-pressed units by way of the river. German forces were unable to penetrate into the area east of the Volga. Those units which had marched so proudly over the Don at the beginning of August made no attempt at all to disrupt supply lines to the defenders of Stalingrad by sending a task force over the Volga--or perhaps they were no longer strong enough to do so.

In the meantime in its third month, the battle for Stalingrad raged on without bringing a decision in the form of incontestable possession of the city. Strangely enough, the battle of Stalingrad failed to remind either Hitler and his advisors or the officers most intimately concerned, Generaloberst von Paulus, Commander in Chief of the Sixth Army, and his General Staff Chief, General Arthur Schmidt, of the action at Verdun in 1916. There, Germany's Western armies were sacrificed on the altar of bloody frontal attack. Memory of Verdun certainly should have served as a warning at Stalingrad. Generaloberst Freiherr von Richthofen, of the Luftwaffe, seemed to be the only one who was unduly disturbed by what was happening at Stalingrad.[46]

Somehow, one cannot escape the feeling that the Germans were paralyzed like rabbits before a snake, in the face of coming events in the East.

After all, had not the Commander in Chief, Luftwaffe, been informed of the fact that a large Russian force was gathering east of the Don River? What did he order in the way of countermeasures?* Is not General Plocher perfectly right when he points out that the establishment of the Luftwaffe Command Don, ostensibly created to come to the aid of von Richthofen's Fourth Air Fleet in the Voronezh area, was approved in reality in order to provide Generaloberst Korten--in high favor with the Luftwaffe High Command--with an appointment as commanding general? Strange that personal vanity could still play a role in the face of the danger approaching from the Russian steppes! According to estimates made by General Plocher,[47] the Luftwaffe High Command could have given the Fourth Air Fleet a few more reinforcements in its battle to hold the Don front, if the Luftwaffe Command Don had not been established for Generaloberst Korten.

To be sure, General Plocher's estimates took even half-groups into account, as, indeed, they had to, for the original estimates made during 1939 and 1940 had been far too low. Germany's armament, as a result, was worse than inadequate. During the Russian campaign Germany simply did not possess the necessary materiel and personnel reserves which must be held in readiness, prepared for immediate action in just such critical situations. Inasmuch as Germany had entrusted Rumanian, Italian, and Hungarian troops with operations on sectors of the front which were of vital importance to the southern wing of the German Army, the least she could have done would have been to provide these troops with effective air cover. Ideally, such cover should have extended far beyond the front into enemy territory, and should have been capable of so dispersing enemy troop assemblies that they had no chance to develop into the serious threat which they represented on 19 November 1942.

The Luftwaffe High Command had administered; it had not led.✝ Apparently it had relied completely on Hitler's proverbial good fortune and on the uncanny intuition which had already brought Germany so many victories. In any case, the Luftwaffe--assigned the mission of providing air cover for the entire southern wing of Germany's Eastern armies in two opposing directions (the Caucasus and Stalingrad), and this with

---

*Actually, in view of the situation, is it not clear that Germany ought to have gathered up every single available aircraft (except those assigned to the Mediterranean, where Rommel's defeat and the Allied landing in November had created an extremely serious situation) for commitment against the coming danger?

✝Plocher, too, notes this discrepancy. See his Study, Book IV, p. 274.

a single air fleet (the Fourth) and the relatively weak Luftwaffe Command Don--found itself in a desperate position between the catastrophe taking place at the bend of the Don and the growing threat of disaster all the way along the line to the Caucasus, where another German army group was already involved in heavy fighting.

Let us outline the individual events very briefly.

The Russian breakthroughs at Serafymovich and Kletskaya on 19 November, followed by successful storming of the line held by the Rumanian Fourth Army south of Stalingrad, resulted in the encirclement of the German Sixth Army, completed by the afternoon of 22 November. The Sixth Army had remarkably little on hand in the way of food, medicine, and ammunition supplies; moreover, although the danger of a Soviet breakthrough along one or both of the Rumanian-held flanks must have been recognized as ever-present, the Sixth Army had made no definite plans to go into effect automatically in the case of such a breakthrough.

The clear-sighted Commander in Chief of Army Group B,* Generalfeldmarschall von Weichs, suggested to Hitler immediately[48] that the Sixth Army should fight its way out of encirclement. It was up to Hitler to make the final decision. Unfortunately, the Sixth Army Command was playing with the idea of digging in for the winter and having itself supplied from the air. In any case, von Weichs' eminently reasonable recommendation for an immediate break out found no clear echo on the part of Sixth Army leaders.

It is totally irrelevant for our study whether it was Reichsmarschall Goering or Luftwaffe General Staff Chief Jeschonnek whom Hitler consulted first in regard to the Luftwaffe's ability to keep Stalingrad supplied from the air. The fact remains that a top-level Luftwaffe commander committed the Luftwaffe to air supply operations for Stalingrad instead of pointing out firmly at the very beginning that such operations could not be carried out.

In the long run, the frightening thing about this decision is that it could have been made without a single qualified dissenter raising

---

*Editor's Note: The Sixth Army, surrounded at Stalingrad, was an element of Army Group B. Later (27 Nov 1942) Army Group Don (Feldmarschall von Manstein) took command of the Sixth Army, the Fourth Panzer Army and the Third Roumanian Army.

his voice. If von Weichs and Zeitzler[*] had found firm and articulate support for their recommendations, then Hitler might have been saved from the pitfall into which he stumbled at Stalingrad--namely the temptation, in his subsequent conduct of the war, to override or ignore the advice of expert counselors.

The Luftwaffe, which, after all, was the agency most affected by the decision, certainly ought to have derived sufficient warning from its earlier air-supply actions at Cholm and Demjansk. It ought to have had on hand, for immediate reference, lists of the losses incurred by those two actions; it ought long since to have prepared a study of all the pros and cons, with appropriate documentation. If this material had been available, the Luftwaffe would have been in a position to give an unqualified and well-documented "no" as answer (unless, of course, an air-supply mission were ordered as a "must"), if Hitler had not been willing to accept a categorical "impossible!" from Goering. We may well ask why the Commander in Chief, Luftwaffe, maintained a military history branch!

The origin of the disaster at Stalingrad, however, was inherent in the personnel make-up of the Luftwaffe long before the Sixth Army was given up for lost. Goering, made uneasy and insecure by Hitler's growing bitterness at the Luftwaffe's failure to stop the highly successful British night raids, was all too easily tempted to promise anything in order to prove that the Luftwaffe was ready and able to perform. Jeschonnek's idealistic concept of the Luftwaffe's highest mission as unreserved obedience to Hitler's will kept him from following the dictates of his own common sense and simply refusing to agree to the Stalingrad operation. Even Generaloberst Freiherr von Richthofen, one of the most realistic men in the Luftwaffe, when he was informed of the decision to attempt what he considered to be an impossible airlift operation, had only the following resigned comment to make: "We have only one chance to cling to; so far the Fuehrer has always been right, even when none of us could understand his actions and most of us had strongly advised against them."[49]

---

*Generaloberst Kurt Zeitzler, Chief of the Army General Staff since Halder's resignation on 24 September 1942, had been firmly against air supply operations from the very beginning, since he considered them completely infeasible. (Generaloberst Zeitzler ueber das Zustandekommen des Entschlusses, Stalingrad aus der Luft zu Versorgen (Generaloberst Zeitzler on the Origin of the Decision to Supply Stalingrad by Airlift), Extract of a letter from General Zeitzler to Professor Suchenwirth, 11 March 1955, G/VI/4d, Karlsruhe Document Collection.)

Despite heroic efforts, the Luftwaffe was unable to keep the promise made by its Commander in Chief. Only one time, on 19 December, did it succeed in bringing as many as 289 tons of supplies into the encircled area with a total of 154 machines.[50] Otherwise the tonnage figures are considerably lower, apart from the fact that there were days on which weather conditions or military developments (such as the catastrophe at Tatsinskaya on 24 December) prevented any aircraft from approaching Stalingrad. The significance of these figures becomes clear when we consider that the Sixth Army needed delivery of 550 tons each day if it was to maintain itself at all.[51] During the period 22 November 1942 through 16 January 1943, an average of approximately 100 tons per day was flown in.[52] If we extend this period to 31 January or 2 February 1943 (the final tragedy of the Sixth Army), the average is even lower—due to loss of the airfields at Pitomnik and Gumrak—despite the untiring energy of Feldmarschall Erhard Milch, who was placed in charge of the Stalingrad airlift on 15 January and given all-encompassing authority to carry it out.

Its heroic efforts in vain, the Luftwaffe lost nearly 500 aircraft (total loss) during the period 24 November 1942 through 2 February 1943. This figure was made up of the following:[53]

266	Ju-52's
42	Ju-86's
165	He-111's
9	FW-200's
5	He-177's
1	Ju-290

Personnel losses amounted to approximately 1,000 men (flight crew personnel).

The VIII Air Corps, previously so successful, met its first defeat in attempting to carry out air supply operations for the encircled Sixth Army. All in all, the Fourth Air Fleet retired from Stalingrad sadly chastened and considerably depleted in strength.

The training program suffered enormously from the loss of aircraft and even more from the loss of qualified instructional personnel, many of whom failed to return. Those officers who had recognized the mission's utter futility from the beginning, but who had had a hand in the tremendous sacrifices made in the desperate effort to accomplish it, were depressed and discouraged beyond words.

*   *   *

Let us consider now just why the catastrophe at Stalingrad, which
resulted in the loss of an entire German army, was a turning point for
the subsequent course of the war, and just why it was so significant
for the Luftwaffe.

Military history contains countless instances in which entire armies
were destroyed without making ultimate victory impossible for their
fatherlands. The Russians themselves, whose armies survived far more
serious catastrophes during 1941, are perhaps the best example of this.
The history of antiquity provides us with still another example, the
Battle of Cannae.

Just what are the factors which determine whether a catastrophe is
to become a link in the chain of ultimate disaster or--as was the case
at Cannae--a first step upwards, towards the winning of the war? The
determining factor would seem to be, more than anything else, the way
in which the catastrophe is received; i.e., what conclusions are drawn
from it.

Let us return to our example of the Battle at Cannae. The reaction
of the Roman Senate and the Roman people to the defeat at Cannae will
always remain one worthy of emulation. Without any loss in dignity,
all possible preparations were made in order to avert the worst effects
of the catastrophe. Steps were taken to mobilize every able-bodied
man; changes were made in the traditional methods of command; a singleness of purpose became apparent in the government of the state. In
short, the Roman people went forth out of the crucible of catastrophe
to a new victory; transformed, hardened, and purified.

As far as Germany was concerned, this is not what happened after
Stalingrad. There were no measures designed to effect total mobilization; the ineffective system of command--whereby officers were manipu-
lated like marionettes from the Rastenburg headquarters--was not curtailed but confirmed. The Stalingrad catastrophe had indeed awakened
Hitler's distrust--unfortunately not towards his own policies but towards
the generals of his armies. Stalingrad could have created a transforma-
tion in Hitler and his military staff; there is no evidence that it did
so.

If Germany's leaders had been cognizant of all the ramifications
of Stalingrad--this strategic error, this source of indescribable
suffering and bitter unhappiness for so many--then they might have
realized that the German people, if properly guided, still had it within

105

their power to develop a tremendous potential energy. At the same time, they might have realized that it was time to turn the Russian campaign into a crusade to liberate the Russian peoples--as well as the Estonians, the Latvians, and the Lithuanians--from Bolshevism. We cannot begin to imagine how far-reaching the effects of such a crusade might have been!

And the Luftwaffe?

Is it possible that Goering and Jeschonnek could have failed to be aware of the urgent necessity for an all-out effort in the air armament and pilot training programs, or of the crying need for the establishment of a reserve force? Must it not have been obvious to them that, without these steps, the Luftwaffe was irrevocably doomed to disintegration? Can they have failed to realize that their only hope lay in being scrupulously realistic in the advice and information they gave to Hitler, even if it meant their becoming personae non gratae? Why did they make no attempt to present their Supreme Commander with tangible documentation of the impossibility of carrying out air-supply operations for the Sixth Army? Why did they not make it absolutely clear to him that the Luftwaffe could not possibly survive another airlift action--especially one which was not really justifiable in point of its potential effectiveness? Would it not have been better for them to risk the loss of prestige and position than permit themselves to become responsible for another costly disaster?

Under existing conditions, such an attitude of self-sacrifice was unthinkable; the spirit prevailing within the Luftwaffe command hierarchy would have to have been an entirely different one. True comradeship and a genuine spirit of leadership would have been possible only if Luftwaffe leaders had succeeded in banishing the prevailing attitude, at best one of indifference and at worst one of active dissatisfaction and dissension. Instead, as the reader may be surprised to learn, precisely during the weeks of the Stalingrad airlift, Jeschonnek and General von Seidel were barely on speaking terms. As a matter of fact, all through the war the Quartermaster General (von Seidel) and the Chief of the Luftwaffe General Staff met only when it was absolutely necessary! Strangely enough Stalingrad was never visited by Goering, Jeschonnek or von Seidel. Instead, from 15 January on, Feldmarschall Milch--placed in charge of all the air-supply operations by Hitler--stood alone at the front, a sort of whipping boy for the others.

Did the Luftwaffe High Command make any changes in its strategic planning as a result of the tragedy at Stalingrad?* There is no

_____
*Especially in view of the fact that Rommel had met defeat in Africa and that the Allies had succeeded in landing there.

evidence that this was the case. Apparently, not even Stalingrad was sufficient to awaken in Luftwaffe leaders a determination to provide Germany with such an impenetrable air cover that her armament program and the lives of her citizens would be safe.

We know that Goering was overcome by a fit of hysterical weeping as the reports of the Stalingrad debacle reached him. This is presumably an indication of the sympathy and, perhaps, guilt which he felt in the face of the sufferings of Germany's soldiers. Far more significant than sympathy, however, would have been a manly deed of resistance, requiring the sacrifice of personal prestige, a willingness to renounce certain comforts and to accept certain inconveniences. The Commander in Chief, Luftwaffe, in his blind selfishness and moral weakness, was incapable of such resistance. Nor did Jeschonnek find in the events at Stalingrad an inspiration to rise above himself and to enforce a spirit of cooperation among Luftwaffe leaders. To be sure, it was late in the day; yet true singleness of purpose might still have saved the Luftwaffe in the crises to come.

In summary, the events at Stalingrad did absolutely nothing to improve, or even to change, the situation existing within the hierarchy of the Luftwaffe command.

Not only did Germany's military leaders fail to draw positive conclusions from the Stalingrad airlift; they even drew some negative ones. And this is what made it an evil omen for Hitler and the Luftwaffe.

Hitler, in his desperate eagerness to prevent the Russians from recapturing any sector of the front for fear that he might lose what territory he had already won, ordered his troops to hold out until it was too late for them to escape encirclement.* And once a force was encircled, he invariably ordered defensive operations to the last man rather than an immediate attempt to break out. It is interesting to observe the changes apparent in the Soviet and German conduct of operations during 1942 and afterwards. During 1941, the Russians sacrificed entire armies to enemy encirclement with the categorical order to hold out at all costs. By the time the Germans launched their summer offensive in 1942, Soviet military leaders had already abandoned this disaster-inviting tactic. Instead, Russian troops learned to withdraw into the depths of their rear area in plenty of time to avoid encirclement. As

------

*Editor's Note: This was not alone a result of Stalingrad, but also a repetition of what Hitler had considered to be his very successful strategy during the winter of 1941-42.

a result, the German advance--although it penetrated quite deeply--did not take nearly so many prisoners as it should have. The same thing was true of the otherwise highly successful German maneuver to recapture the city of Kharkov in 1943. While the Russians tended more and more towards greater mobility in their conduct of operations, German military policy became steadily less flexible after Stalingrad.

And what about the Luftwaffe?

Hitler never reproached Goering publicly for the fact that he was the one responsible for Stalingrad; still, if Goering had not given his casual assurance that air-supply operations were feasible, then Hitler would probably not have issued his fatal order to the Sixth Army to hold out.[54] Although he did not make a public issue out of it, Hitler's faith in the good judgment of his erstwhile first advisor had suffered still another setback. Goering's reaction was to become even more immediately acquiescent to Hitler's every whim in a desperate effort to regain the latter's confidence. His original independence of mind was replaced by complete intellectual submission to the Fuehrer, until he was soon nothing more than "his master's voice," as the last General Staff Chief called him.[55] It is obvious that a yes-man like Goering could not protect the already exhausted Luftwaffe from being exploited beyond the point of endurance.

Goering's reaction to the Stalingrad catastrophe, then, was diametrically opposed to what it ought to have been. Instead of taking counsel with his conscience and resolving to make up for his years of neglect by settling down to intensive and intelligent work, he persisted in his attitudes of absolute submissiveness towards Hitler and nagging jealousy towards Jeschonnek, and permitted nothing to interfere with the continuance of his own comfortable existence, untouched by the exigencies of war. The seeds of disaster, sown long ago, were beginning to bear fruit.

"God is just!," as Wallenstein is supposed to have exclaimed in 1643 when he received the news that his plot had failed. One is tempted to say the same about the outcome of World War II, especially when one considers the way in which Hitler and Goering reacted to Stalingrad--the last possible warning--by compounding the errors which they had already made.

VI - The Lost Fighter Battle[56]

When the Battle of Britain was broken off, German air warfare in the West was already on the defensive. To be sure, those few night-fighter units still available for home air defense operations were able to combat the British attackers successfully, although the latter had already begun (in July 1941) area bombardment on residential sections with incendiary bombs. The British attacked in waves, the participating aircraft carrying out individual bomber runs during both the approach and departure flights. As long as the British continued to utilize these tactics, General Josef Kammhuber, chief of Germany's night-fighter operations, was able to combat them to a certain extent with the "four-poster" method, whereby the fighter aircraft were stationed in air standby areas and were then directed from ground radar stations to the enemy bombers. Thanks to Kammhuber's night fighters, the Royal Air Force--despite its delivered bomb load of 35,000 tons--could not book a total success for 1941.

The German night fighters were employed in a line extending from the island of Sylt to the mouth of the Scheldt River, ranged in front of the antiaircraft batteries. Enemy aircraft approaching over Holland automatically ran into some nine to twelve night-fighter stations. Since this was too little to be really effective, at the end of 1941 an attempt was made at combined night-fighter operations, i.e. the integration of fighter aircraft and searchlights within a tightly limited area, the whole directed from a central ground station. Sixteen of the stations along the Sylt-Scheldt line were utilized for "dark-night" operations; a belt of stations immediately behind this line (thus stretching from the Danish border to Aix la Chapelle), as well as a number ranged before Berlin, carried out "illuminated night-fighter operations;" and a total of nine stations were committed in the combined operations described above. The limitations of this system became obvious, of course, as soon as the enemy was in a position to send over a really sizable bomber fleet. For example, only thirty-six night-fighter aircraft could be employed over the Ruhr District in accordance with the methods outlined. And it could hardly be expected that each one of these thirty-six would manage to down an enemy bomber, though, on the other hand, there were fighter aces who chalked up several kills for each mission. In any case, there was no doubt but that the number of fighter aircraft employed was not sufficient to inflict more than token damage (less than 15%) on an enemy who was even fairly strong.

The night-fighter command directed a goodly number of recommendations to the Commander in Chief, Luftwaffe, most of them requiring an unrealistic increase in the available production facilities and none of them capable of immediate fulfillment. For the cost of any one of the suggested projects the night-fighter command could have financed the operations of at least two more aircraft from each stand-by sector. It is open to question whether any one of the recommendations would have resulted in a substantial increase in the number of enemy bombers downed.

Long-range fighter operations (i.e. fighter operations over British airfields) were carried out by the I Group and 4th Squadron, 2d Night Fighter Wing, during 1941, until the transfer of the I Group to the Mediterranean made continuation impossible. Hitler was not particularly impressed with the potential effectiveness of such operations--quite apart from the fact that they could have little or no value in bolstering civilian morale, inasmuch as they could not easily be followed from Germany. After a short period of experimentation, these operations were discontinued, though General Kammhuber was personally convinced of their potential efficacy.

General Grabmann has the following to say in this connection:[57]

> In view of the highly complicated and weather-
> sensitive take-off and landing maneuvers practiced
> by the Royal Air Force in its steadily increasing
> nocturnal bombardment activity, a well-developed
> system of German long-range fighter pursuit would
> have had an excellent chance of success. The fact
> that Germany neglected to develop this weapon as
> long as she had the chance to do so must be counted
> as one of the gravest sins of omission on the part
> of the night fighter command.

Britain, as a result of such sins of omission, was able to build up her strength without interference.

Although British air attacks during 1941 could not be counted entirely successful, in the spring of 1942 the Royal Air Force brought off a successful area bombardment raid on Luebeck (during the night of 28/29 April), which was followed by several similar attacks on Rostock. The night attack on Cologne (30/31 May), carried out by some 1,000 British bombers, was alarmingly effective, as were the subsequent attacks on Essen (on 1 June) and Luebeck (25 June). German night fighter defenses at Cologne accounted for no more than thirty-six British bombers--slightly more than 3% of the attacking force. This was hardly a record which could be expected to deter a stubborn, strongly-industrialized enemy from further attacks. There was no doubt but what German night fighter operations were sadly ineffective.

It is completely beyond comprehension that Goering, faced with the mounting effectiveness of the RAF raids, failed to insist upon the immediate issuance (by the Commander in Chief, Armed Forces) of special instructions designed to achieve a rapid and disproportionately large increase in Germany's manufacture of air armament equipment. On the other hand, since Germany's bombers were committed on the Eastern front, Hitler's policy of meeting terror with terror could only be implemented sporadically. Under these conditions, Germany's raids against England gradually disintegrated into pinpricks, or what the British called "baby blitzes." Thus, Germany's only hope lay in a strengthening of her antiaircraft defenses--including the fighter aircraft arm--especially since the intervention of American bomber units was obviously imminent. Fighter aircraft and modern radar equipment were the answer! Yet in 1941 Jeschonnek declined Milch's offer to raise fighter production to 1,000 units per month. The General Staff Chief explained that he had no use for more than 360 per month, since he had only 170 crews to man them.

*   *   *

At this point let us dispel an **illusion inherent in the term so** often applied to Germany's part in World War II; the term in question is "the poor man's war." It can only be used accurately, however, when comparing Germany, with a power like the United States. Germany's potential was not inconsiderable; however--and this is a point which is all too frequently ignored--it did not develop completely until it was too late for it to be effective. Armaments production, for example, reached its peak during the first six to eight months of 1944 (July and August were the peak period).* If the same goals could have been attained during the first half of 1942, then Russia would have been very hard put to maintain herself in the air and at sea, and an Allied invasion of France--despite America's military might--would never have been possible. We must not forget that a full mobilization of Germany's armament potential in 1942 (and such mobilization was within the realm of possibility) would have resulted in a very considerable increase in overall war potential during the following years. One neglected opportunity after another, including the chance at a negotiated peace.⌿

---

*Hans Kehrl states the following: "The armament production slated for allocation to the Army would have been sufficient to re-equip 225 infantry divisions from the ground up and to equip 45 newly-activated armored divisions." (Bilanz des Zweiten Weltkriegs (The Balance Sheet of World War II), Hans Kehrl, "Kriegswirtschaft und Kriegsindustrie" (Military Economy and the War Industry), Gerhard Stalling, (Hamburg, 1953), p. 282.)

⌿The Allied decision to insist on unconditional surrender was not announced until January 1943.

We know, at least to some extent, why these opportunities were not utilized. In the armament industry, for example, Udet and Todt did not have anywhere near the same degree of influence as did their successors, Milch (for the Luftwaffe) and Speer and Saur (for all other armament sectors). In addition, the many requests for special weapons development prevented the Speer ministry from turning its attention to conventional armament programs, including that of the Luftwaffe, until 1944. As far as command was concerned, Germany's military leaders simply failed to see the possibilities inherent in strategic air warfare against Russia and they completely ignored the necessity of building a strong fighter aircraft arm for employment in home air defense operations.

The story behind these two wholly inexplicable errors is one of the most perplexing cases of self-delusion in all history.

First, right after the beginning of the Polish campaign, Hitler was still hopeful that England and France would not declare war on Germany. Second, once the Polish campaign was concluded, Hitler was firmly convinced that England would be ready to sue for peace, inasmuch as a final decision had been reached (i.e. the territories in question—about half of Poland—were in German hands) and the motivation for the war had been removed—further bloodshed was unnecessary. Third, after the conspicuous success of the campaign in the West, evidenced by France's capitulation, Germany's leaders were convinced that the war was already won, that England could finally be forced to make peace, and that this goal could be achieved by any nation willing to sanction the continued existence of the British Empire (and Hitler felt that the empire should be preserved). Thrice the victim of self-delusionment, Hitler clung ever more firmly to the conviction (which was soon to become an obsession) that Germany had already won the war, including the war against Russia—and this despite the setbacks suffered during December 1941. Firm in his belief that the German offensive in the summer of 1942 (which really seemed to be off to an excellent start) would bring about the final collapse of Soviet Russia, it is quite probable that Hitler and his devoted disciples (and this group very definitely included Jeschonnek, Chief of the Luftwaffe General Staff) really believed that the German bombers would return victorious from the East to avenge the injuries inflicted by the British night raids and to make further offensive operations by the English impossible.

In summary, Germany's leaders were first betrayed into inaction by their unrealistic hope for peace, nurtured far too long; afterwards they were so blinded by rapid and relatively effortless victory that they failed to take advantage of the time given them for armaments

112

production. As a result, Germany simply drifted along, her leaders always convinced that final victory was imminent, until they found themselves suddenly on the brink of disaster. By the time they recognized the peril and plunged the nation into hectic armament activity in an effort to make up for lost time, it was already too late.

It was not the poor man who lost the war, but rather the man who refused to face reality.

*   *   *

The British tactic of the bomber stream was the undoing of Germany's night fighter defense system. During 1942 England carried out a total of seventeen large-scale attacks. And on 17 August 1942 came the first daylight attack by American four-engine bombers. The American aircraft had particularly efficient armaments in the tail region, which was the "classical" point of attack for a fighter aircraft.

The daylight attacks, of course, represented a far greater danger to Germany's antiaircraft defenses than the night raids. The majority of the former were carefully planned attacks--like the first of its type, on 27 January 1943--and since the bombers travelled in close formation, it was extremely difficult for the German fighters to get in near enough to strike an effective blow against the heavily armed and heavily armored B-17's and B-24's. Needless to say, American losses were very slight.

The American system of target selection was fairly predictable, and the American attacks--insofar as their targets lent themselves to nocturnal bombardment--were usually followed up by British raids, carried out as area bombardment missions by bomber aircraft guided by the path-finding Mosquitos. The German submarine arm was the first top-priority target for the Americans--submarine bases, factories, diesel engine works, and shipyards. The German aircraft industry, including auxiliary parts factories, ball-bearing works, and assembly plants, was the next one. This was followed by the Ruhr District, various rail centers, and finally Berlin (because of its electrical industry).

Only after a great deal of experimentation were the German fighter aircraft able to work out an effective method of attack for use against the four-engine bombers. In recognition of the serious threat represented by these bombers, it was decided, in July 1943, to replace the single-engine fighter units on the Western, Eastern, and Southern fronts with twin-engine fighter units. The single-engine fighters were then to be used to reinforce the home air defense units. It was high time.

113

The British raid on Hamburg (24/25 July), which was followed by an American daylight attack (an effective technique, incidentally, and one which the Allies often employed throughout July), resulted in very serious damage to the Hanseatic city. In addition, the British succeeded in paralyzing the German night-fighter and antiaircraft defenses by jamming their radar equipment with aluminum-foil strips (the process known as "dueppling,"* after the village of Dueppel). Gradually, the night-fighter forces learned to function effectively in spite of enemy jamming; the antiaircraft artillery, however, dependent upon its electrical aiming equipment, never fully recovered.

On 17 August, the German day-fighter forces (somewhat increased in the meantime) succeeded in bringing down at least sixty of the 315 American bombers participating in an attack on the ball-bearing works at Schweinfurt; as a result the enemy refrained from attack for ten days. This minor success was sufficient to awaken the optimism of Goering and Milch, without, however, inspiring them to do everything possible to preserve Germany's new-found defensive strength at its present level by introducing measures designed to increase aircraft production (such as the 72-hour week). The peak of day-fighter effectiveness was reached on 14 October 1943, when sixty-six out of an attacking force of 295 B-17's were shot down over Schweinfurt. The October average for enemy aircraft downed was 12.4%, contrasted with a loss of only 4% for the defending fighters. Even during this peak month, the minimum figure of 15% was not attained. And from November on, the situation changed radically. The enemy began to schedule his attacks for periods of bad weather, having noticed that the German fighters (due to the lack of adequate pilot training in instrument flight) were completely helpless. In addition, the American bombers were often escorted by heavily-armed long-range fighter aircraft whose radius of operations soon covered the entire German Reich. Not only were the England-based bombers of the American Eighth Air Force becoming more and more dangerous, but towards the end of 1943 Germany began to notice the effects of the assignment of the American Fifteenth Air Force to the Italian airfields at Foggia (captured by the Allies on 28 September). From the Italian bases, the American bombers were able to attack southern Germany and the eastern portions of the Reich, as well as targets located in the Balkans. This served to dissipate German air defense forces even further.

The German single-engine fighter aircraft were incapable (as a result of the inadequate training of their pilots on the one hand and

---

*Termed "window" or "chaff" by the Allies.

the inadequacy of their equipment on the other) of attacking in close formation an enemy bomber stream approaching above a closed cloud cover. Nor was it possible for the twin-engine fighters to be effective in an attack of this kind. Moreover, German antiaircraft artillery was fairly useless in view of the flight altitude of the enemy bombers, quite apart from the fact that its instruments were extremely vulnerable to enemy jamming.

Thus, in 1944, the German fighter aircraft forces were unable to combat effectively the enemy air attacks, which were systematically directed towards the destruction of the sources of German military strength. This was true in the case of the February attacks on the factories producing airframes, as well as of the carefully planned attacks--begun in the spring and continued relentlessly--on the gasoline hydration plants in central and eastern Germany.

Beginning with the American bomber attacks in 1944, with their strong fighter escorts, Germany's day fighter defenses were doomed to operations which resulted in heavy losses and yet failed to inflict any appreciable damage. The night fighter forces were in an equally critical position, since the British bomber stream tactic had robbed the "four-poster" method of its effectiveness. Moreover, the British jamming of radar equipment, as introduced during the attack on Hamburg, presented a very serious problem.

In this situation Goering was willing to grasp at any straw. The first was a suggestion made by Major Hajo Hermann on 27 June 1943 concerning the possibility of illuminated night fighter operations. These were to be operations by single-engine fighters, utilizing the illumination provided at the scene of attack by burning buildings as well as searchlights to simulate daylight conditions and thus to obviate the danger of "window." In spite of initial successes, this method did not continue to justify the hopes placed upon it. On the other hand, realization of a suggestion made on 29 July 1943 by Colonel von Lossberg proved to be of great assistance to Germany's night fighter forces. Basing his recommendations on a study by Major (Engineer) Guenther of the Technical Office, von Lossberg suggested that the night fighters should infiltrate the enemy bomber stream during the approach and return flights, should be reinforced as much as possible, and should then carry out individual pursuit operations. By combining Hermann's and von Lossberg's suggestions within the framework of the "four-poster" method, it ought to have been possible to guide three times as many fighters against the enemy bomber stream. Lossberg's method of individual pursuit was most successful during the British attack on Nuremberg on the night of 30/31 March 1944, when a total of 107 bombers was

115

shot down,* a record which had never before been achieved and which was never again to be equalled, even by the day-fighter forces. This "triumph of the pursuit method"[58] was possible only because the majority of the night-fighter aircraft were equipped with the Li-SN-2 radar instrument. The enemy, however, far superior to Germany in the development of radar equipment, continually invented new methods of jamming German radar. By October 1944, the British had found a way to jam the SN-2 completely, and German night fighter operations were on the wane. During October the night fighters managed to destroy only 6.6% of attacking enemy aircraft; in November the figure dropped to 1½%; in December to 0.7%; in January it rose to 1.3%; and in February dropped back to 1.2%. Needless to say, these losses were insignificant for the enemy. During the month of March, the gasoline shortage was so acute that only top-ranking crews were permitted to fly. Operation GISELA, during the night of 4/5 March, represented one last success for the German night fighter forces. In carefully planned operations, the fighters slipped into the enemy bomber stream and by individual pursuit and aerial combat over Chemnitz (the scene of the attack) they managed to bring down seventy-five four-engine bombers.

We may well ask whether German military leaders made any attempt in early 1944 to create more favorable conditions for the day-fighter forces. Chief of Procurement and Supply Milch certainly made every effort to support the hard-pressed day-fighter units by increasing aircraft production as much as he could. On 1 March 1944, when it seemed clear that the February air attacks had almost completely destroyed the German aircraft industry, one last attempt was made to save the situation by the establishment of the Fighter Staff. Its missions were the reconstruction of the industrial facilities destroyed by the enemy, the achievement of the fighter production goal established by Milch in 1943, and the removal of air armament works to safer, underground locations. This entire project was entrusted to Saur, Speer's most powerful assistant, and was given top priority. Soon thereafter, the Luftwaffe armament program was made an integral part of the activity of Speer's ministry. As usual, purposeful action came far too late.

Even so, the Fighter Staff did manage to bring about a considerable

---

*Editor's Note: The British estimated their losses at 94 bombers. (Hilary St. George Saunders, Royal Air Force, 1939-1945, Vol. III, The Fight is Won, Her Majesty's Stationery Office, (London, 1954), p. 28.)

increase in the production of single-engine fighter aircraft.* However, the fighter forces were still restricted to traditional models, which—despite the gradual improvements being made in them—were no match for the enemy. This might not have been the case if Hitler had not obstructed for so long the development of the Me-262,† and if Milch had supported—in time—the further development of the Do-325, a new Dornier fighter with a speed of 435 miles, which never reached the mass production stage. An increase in fighter production was no longer sufficient, and an increase in quality was apparently either beyond Germany's capabilities or came too late to be of any use.

Obviously, the production of thousands of single-engine fighter aircraft made a difference in the operational readiness of Germany's fighter arm. On 2 November 1944, for example, there were 695 day fighters available for employment, and on 28 November, 684 night fighters. These figures represented the climax in operational readiness for the fighter forces.

The German fighter pilot's inferiority to his American counterpart—in number, in the standard of the training he had been given,[59] and in the performance qualities of his aircraft—was bound to have an unfavorable effect on his morale, particularly since he knew his often heroic efforts were wholly unappreciated by Goering. This may well have been one of the reasons for the Luftwaffe's failure to increase its strength materially in spite of the tremendous rise in aircraft production figures during the period of the Fighter Staff. Another reason for this failure can be traced to Germany's highest-level commanders who were making plans which were to result in the dissolution of the reserve force which had been slowly building up and which the General of the Fighter Forces planned to utilize in a large-scale offensive against the American bomber streams. The first such instance was in June 1944, when the Allies landed in France. Hitler ordered the majority of the fighter forces to France, where the successes they achieved were really insignificant in terms of overall events, but where their lack of familiarity with the airfields and the difficult conditions under which they were forced to operate against an enemy far superior in number caused

---

*See footnote 3, Chapt. 2. The highest production figure achieved was 3,129 (including the Me-262 and the fighter-interceptor Me-163), in September 1944. (Figures are based on Werner Baumbach, Zu Spaet; Aufstieg und Untergang der deutschen Luftwaffe (Too Late; The Rise and Fall of the Luftwaffe), Richard Pflaum, (Munich, 1949), p. 78.)

†See below, Section VIII.

117

enormously high losses.

The second instance of such wasteful employment occurred during
the Ardennes offensive. This ambitious operation had been carefully
prepared. With Goering's concurrence, plans had been made to withdraw
the day-fighter units from action long enough for their personnel and
materiel strength to be restored. As soon as this point had been
reached, and weather conditions were favorable, a force of 2,000 single-
engine fighters were to be sent up in aerial combat against the enemy
in the hope of inflicting such heavy losses that the Allies would
refrain from further strategic air operations. As a tentative goal,
the destruction of 400-500 four-engine bombers and at least as many
enemy fighters had been established. The Luftwaffe had completed its
preparations by the first week in November, and Goering had even addressed
a personal appeal to the fighter forces (7 November). Then, in contradiction to these plans and in spite of vigorous protests on the part
of Galland, Hitler ordered the fighter forces to be transferred to the
Western theater for employment in the Ardennes offensive. Weather conditions were extremely unfavorable for fighter operations; losses were
high and success nil.

The third instance, Operation BODENPLATTE (Ground Plate), carried
out on 1 January 1945 and directed against fifteen Allied airfields in
France, Holland, and Belgium, used up what was left of the reserve
force. In a surprise attack costing 150 German fighter aircraft and
their crews, the Luftwaffe managed to destroy 800 enemy machines on the
ground. Grabmann calls it "a Pyrrhic victory paid for by destruction
of the last reserves of the Luftwaffe."*

Understandably, from this point on the day-fighter forces played a
fairly insignificant role. The Me-262, which was finally ready for front
operations, was utilized with good success. On 18 March, for example,
a force of thirty-seven Me 262's was sent up against 1,200 American
four-engine bombers flying with fighter escort; in spite of very bad
weather conditions, the Me-262's made thirteen sure kills and two prob-
ables, while losing only two of their own machines. The growing effectiveness of enemy fighter operations, however, was already making it difficult for the German jet fighters to take off without interference, and
this became more and more of a problem as the borders of the Reich
shrank before the advance of enemy armies from the East and West. Had
this new weapon been available one year earlier, it would certainly have
brought about a fundamental change in the air situation. As it was, the

_____

*Grabmann's figure for the number of enemy aircraft destroyed may
be somewhat high.

Me-262 was consigned to destruction on the ground because the long runways it needed for take-off could no longer be adequately protected.

One must admire the stubborn tenacity of the Luftwaffe leaders in continuing the battle against an overwhelmingly superior enemy air force until the last aircraft and last drop of gasoline had been expended. Actually, the battle was lost at that moment when Hitler interfered in the development of the Me-262--a project which should have had the very highest priority--with the result that its production was delayed until it was too late.

VII - The Last Opportunity - The Jet Fighter

The moment the American long-range fighters were in a position to escort the American, and then the British, bomber streams to any target in German-held territory, it was clear that the German fighter forces faced certain defeat if they continued to utilize traditional aircraft models and equipment. The only instrument capable of effectively meeting the enemy onslaught (which threatened to annihilate Germany sooner or later) was a jet fighter aircraft with a substantially higher rate of speed than that of the enemy fighters.

It will always remain one of the inexplicable puzzles of World War II that Germany had just such a weapon within her grasp, and that the inconceivable blindness of her top-level leaders resulted in a six-months' delay in its release for production--coming on top of the developmental delays already occasioned by high-level indecisiveness and exaggerated caution.

Even before the beginning of the war, the Heinkel plant had begun to work in this--at that time--futuristic direction. Its He-178, as a matter of fact, had already been tested on 24 and 27 August 1939. During the course of the war, Heinkel developed a twin-engine jet fighter, which was tried out for the first time in 1941. Messerschmitt, however, with his designs for the Me-262, forged ahead of the Heinkel works, which then retired from the jet fighter race. One of Messerschmitt's experimental models had already passed two tests on the efficiency of its jet motors (although, in the interests of safety, a conventional piston engine had been installed in the gunner's cockpit). During the spring or summer of 1941,[*] when Messerschmitt reported to

---

*". . . at a time when Udet's star was already setting . . .," as Messerschmitt states in a letter to Generalmajor a. D. Walter Grabmann. Our description of the visit is also based on this letter. (Ltr. Willy Messerschmitt to Walter Grabmann, 24 Aug 55, copy in C/IV/2bb, Karlsruhe Document Collection.)

Udet and Milch on the progress of the Me-262, the latter refused to order a speed-up in developmental work, despite Messerschmitt's warning that England or America might be working in the same direction. "If they decide to concentrate on development of jet-propelled aircraft," Messerschmitt is supposed to have said, "it could easily mean catastrophe for Germany."

The refusal on the part of Luftwaffe leaders to push the development of his Me-262 did not distrub Messerschmitt too much; he continued with his experimentation. Taking care to move "as secretly as possible," he had already made arrangements with the Junkers and BMW engine works to go ahead with development of the jet engines. By mid-1942, according to its creator, the Me-262 had already been flown as a jet aircraft without piston engine.[60]

Soon afterwards, a Major Opitz applied for and received permission from Messerschmitt to try out the Me-262. His reaction was one of unqualified enthusiasm. Through him, Galland was led to fly the machine himself, which he did in April and again on 22 May 1943. Three days later, he reported the following to the Reichsmarshall:[61]

1. This model is a tremendous stroke of luck for us; it puts us way out in front, provided the enemy continues to utilize piston engines.

2. As far as I could tell, the fuselage seems to be entirely satisfactory.

3. The engines are everything which has been claimed for them, except for their performance during take-off and landing.

4. The aircraft opens up entirely new possibilities as far as tactics are concerned.

Galland recommended that production of the Me-209 be discontinued, inasmuch as the FW-190-D, which was as good if not better than the Me-209 in all respects, was rapidly being developed. He suggested that single-engine fighter production should be limited to the FW-190 in future, some of them equipped with the BMW-801 engine and others with the DB-603. He goes on to urge that "the production capacity thus freed" should be "switched to the Me-262 program."[62]

In a meeting conducted by the Chief of Procurement and Supply on 2 June 1943, it was decided to release the Me-262 for series production

"because of its superior speed as well as its many other qualities."[63]
On 17 August 1943, when Milch announced a fighter production goal of
4,000 per month (calculated to raise 1944's fighter readiness to an
unprecedented peak), Galland demanded that 1,000 of them be jet fighters.
Milch demurred, however, explaining that he could not be expected to
stop all other developmental projects just because of the Me-262. He
continued, "the Fuehrer feels that the risk is too great . . . . I,
personally, would go ahead and produce it, as we had planned, without
all this business of discontinuing the Me-209. However, as a soldier
I have no choice but to obey orders. If the Fuehrer orders caution,
then we must be cautious." Milch's statement, based on stenographic
notes,[64] flatly contradicts information provided by Galland to the
effect that the Fuehrer had ordered full-capacity production of the
Me-262 in the early spring of 1943, and that all the necessary preparations had been made. According to Galland, the Messerschmitt works
were obviously too poorly organized to carry out this order, since they
were continually getting into difficulty by failure to meet delivery
dates.[65]

One fact seems sure; the Technical Office hesitated far too long,
partly in memory of previous disappointments and partly in its inability
to break away from tradition. Galland was the one who kept calling for
action; finally, Hitler intervened, but unfortunately--tragically for
the exciting potentialities of the new model--to demand an impossible
(at first, anyway) modification.

On 2 November, Hitler sent Goering to the Messerschmitt plant at
Augsburg in order to broach the question of equipping the Me-262 to
carry bombs.[66] Messerschmitt replied that the original plans had always
envisioned the installation of two bomb release clips, for either two
550-lb. bombs or one 1,100-lb. one. This equipment, however, including
the necessary wiring, had not yet been installed because the machine
was being prepared for mass production. Pleasantly surprised, Goering
assured him that this was all the Fuehrer wanted to know. The Fuehrer
wanted the aircraft to carry a bomb load of two 154-lb. bombs; if it
could manage two 550-lb. bombs, so much the better. Goering then asked
how soon the first models would be ready. Faced with a direct question
such as this, Messerschmitt had no choice but to admit the truth--the
bomb release clips had not yet been designed.* As soon as the design

_____

*According to Baumbach, "The discrepancies and self-contradictions
present in Messerschmitt's reports are indicative of the argumentation
and deceit which had become common in reports intended for Goering's
ears or eyes. Goering was far too gullible to realize that Messerschmitt
was only playing for time in the face of the sudden demand that he establish definite deadlines." (Baumbach, Werner, Zu Spaet, (Too Late),
Richard Pflaum, (Munich, 1949), p. 93.)

could be finished, there would be no difficulty in installing them in the test models. Goering's next words to Messerschmitt hit the nail on the head: "You stated that the original plans envisioned the installation of bomb release clips; surely that must mean that you've given the problem some study!" Messerschmitt replied that all the data were included in the appendix to the construction plans. Again the Reichsmarschall touched upon a sore point when he inquired exactly how great the delay would be "in case of dire emergency." Messerschmitt's reply was casual--one is tempted to term it criminally casual--"Oh, not very long - two weeks, perhaps. It isn't really much of a problem; just a matter of camouflaging the clips." Goering continued with a question as to how many machines were available for testing, to which Messerschmitt replied that none from the latest production series was ready as yet. The model had been designed in 1938 and flown for the first time in 1941. It was obvious that the production guidelines had needed revision. At the present time, there was one experimental model available; there would have been more but for the fact that one had been totally destroyed in a crash landing and two others seriously damaged. Messerschmitt went on to say that one model had been constructed on a stable nosewheel, but that its take-off and landing performance seemed to be no better than that of a normal machine.[67]

On 2 November, a special commission was established under Colonel Petersen to guide the development of the Me-262.* The Chief of Procurement and Supply was beginning to be seriously concerned at the manpower which was being requisitioned for work on the fuselage, engines, and equipment of the new model. On 12 November 1943 Milch asked for Vorwald's opinion of the following question: "The one thing we are not yet entirely sure of is the problem of whether the Me-262, with its jet engines, is so foolproof that we can go ahead with production next year. Are we ready--not only in point of development but also in point of production?" Vorwald's answer was an unqualified "yes!" Major Knemeyer, on the other hand, warned of the catastrophic situation in the Messerschmitt plant, where everything had run into a bottleneck.[68] On

---

*The other members were Dr. Werner and Director Frydag of the Industry Council, General (Engineer) Sellschopp, Captain (Engineer) Kaufmann, Major Knemeyer, General (Engineer) Mahnke, and Colonel (Engineer) Alpers from the Luftwaffe, and Professor Messerschmitt, Director Hentzen, Engineer Bley, Director Cambeis, and Director Franz von Jumo. (Fernschreiben Milch an Reichsmarschall, Gst. Nr. 1587/43 g. Kdos. (Teletype, Milch to Reichsmarschall, General Staff No. 1587/43, Classified), C/IV/2bb, Karlsruhe Document Collection.)

30 November, the Chief of Procurement and Supply complained bitterly of the delays in delivery, and of the juggling of numbers, dates, and deadlines by the Messerschmitt firm.[69]

Soon Hitler's own influence in the affair of the Me-262 became apparent. In a telegram to the Reichsmarschall, dated 5 December 1943 and signed by Hitler's Luftwaffe aide, the following appears:[70]

> The Fuehrer has called our attention once more to the tremendous importance of the production of jet propelled aircraft for employment as fighter-bombers. It is imperative that the Luftwaffe have a number of jet fighter-bombers ready for front commitment by the spring of 1944. Any difficulties occasioned by labor and raw material shortages will be resolved by the exploitation of Luftwaffe resources, until such time as existing shortages can be made up. The Fuehrer feels that a delay in our jet fighter program would be tantamount to irresponsible negligence. The Fuehrer has directed that bimontly written reports, the first due on 15 November 1943, be made to him concerning the program of the Me-262 and the Arado-234.

The above gives us a clear indication of just what Hitler had in mind. The Me-262 was to be a fighter-bomber. In a conversation with Milch on 5 January 1944, he emphasized once more that he needed jet bombers and modern submarines in order to meet the expected Allied invasion.[71]

Under the circumstances, it is easy to visualize Hitler's rage and disappointment when he learned in April 1944 (on the occasion of a conference with Milch, Fighter Staff Chief Saur, and Goering) that the Me-262 was not being built to carry bombs. Thoroughly upset, he shouted: "Not a single one of my orders has been obeyed!" Milch's comment that the Me-262 was designed to be a fighter, and not a bomber, did nothing to placate the Fuehrer's rage, but did serve to weaken Milch's prestige.[72]

Goering, who--once upon a time--had maintained a certain degree of independence towards Hitler (as evidenced by his having dared to advise him against the Russian campaign), had been brought through the many failures suffered by his Luftwaffe to the point where he was no longer morally capable of an energetic protest, bolstered by the threat of his resignation. Hitler, angry, feeling betrayed and stubbornly insisting on the need for a "blitz bomber," saw, in the Reichsmarschall, someone

who no longer needed to be taken seriously, who might be buffeted about
at will. Goering's authority was gone; his original independence of
thought had been replaced by an exaggerated, abject obedience which he
hoped, would permit him to maintain his position.

Goering's attitude was clearly illustrated during the May conference
on the Obersalzberg.* On 29 May, immediately after the talks were concluded, Goering spoke to a group consisting of Messerschmitt, Bodenschatz, Petersen, Galland, Korten, etc.,[73] "In order to avoid a mislead-
ing designation, I suggest that we call the new aircraft a 'super-speed
bomber,'/ rather than a fighter-bomber. Accordingly, the further
development of this model will be entrusted to the General of the Bomber
Forces." The Fuehrer would decide "which of those experimental models
equipped with armaments should be developed further as fighter aircraft."
This is confirmed by Bodenschatz, when he says, "The Fuehrer ordered
expressly that its development as a fighter should be continued."
Galland, arriving on the scene, was informed by the Reichsmarschall
that ". . . it is not that the Fuehrer wants the new model to be only
a bomber - quite the contrary, he is aware of its potentialities as a
fighter. However, he does want all of those presently in production
to come out as super-speed bombers until further notice. It is his
desire that we concentrate on the bomber question and that the problems
of bomb-carrying capacity, bomb release clip design, bombsight development, and bombardment tactics be given paramount consideration." Goering went on to explain that the super-speed bomber might be used in the
coming invasion, ". . . on the English coast, for example, to bombard
the beach while the invasion force was going aboard and the boats and
already landed equipment during unloading operations. As I see it, our
aircraft would fly along the beach, dropping their bombs into the confusion below. This is the way in which the Fuehrer envisions employment of the new model, and this is the way it will be!" The Reichsmarschall was afraid of incurring Hitler's wrath again; once, during
the course of the subsequent conversation, Messerschmitt inadvertently
used the word "fighter" in conjunction with the Me-262, and was interrupted immediately by Goering with the words, "Will you please stop
using that word 'fighter'!" The Reichsmarschall almost begged those

---

*Editor's Note: In the vicinity of Berchtesgaden. Hitler, Goering,
Bormann, Speer and a number of other prominent Nazis had homes on the
Obersalzberg.

/Editor's Note: Usually referred to as "Blitz Bomber," the Me-262
was also called "high-speed bomber," "jet bomber," etc.

present to do nothing behind his back which might upset his plans. "The commands of the Fuehrer must remain inviolable!"

The minutes of a discussion between Hitler and Saur on 7 June 1944 confirm the Fuehrer's demands in connection with the new aircraft model.* All attempts to change his mind were of no avail. Armaments Minister Speer tried it and failed; on 30 August, General Kreipe, sixth Chief of the Luftwaffe General Staff, tried his luck and did manage to obtain one minor concession--that every twentieth Me-262 would be equipped as a fighter.[74] Hitler did not give final permission to begin series production of the Me-262 as a fighter until 4 November 1944, and even then he stipulated that each aircraft "must be able to carry at least one 550-lb. bomb in case of emergency."[75]

The dates mentioned in the foregoing are enough to tell us that there was no chance of Germany's having her super-speed bomber ready in time for the Allied landing in Northern France. On 22 June, at a meeting of the Fighter Staff, Saur lectured his colleagues:[76]

> . . . we deserve to be soundly reproached;
> during September and October of last year we
> made certain promises which we based not on
> fact but on pure wishful thinking. We simply
> assumed that we would have a goodly number of
> machines available for rigorous testing by Janu-
> ary or February; we assumed that we would produce
> at least thirty to forty aircraft during March,
> sixty per month by May, and soon thereafter seventy-
> five to eighty per month. It is now June, and we do
> not have one single machine. We have only ourselves
> to blame--we were incapable of finding the necessary
> resources, incapable of concentrating our efforts,
> and incapable of approaching the problem with the

---

*Initial production of the Me-262 was to be limited to the bomber. Testing of the fighter might continue, but ". . . under no circumstances is bomber production to be delayed while waiting for the results of such tests . . . . Not until these tests have been concluded and their results evaluated will fighter production be permitted to start. Once this point has been reached, there is no reason why production capacity cannot be divided between the two models." (Besprechung beim Fuehrer, 7. Juni 1944, Saur, Protokoll vom 8. 6. 1944 (Conference with the Fuehrer, 7 June 1944, Saur, protocol of 8 June 1944), C/VI/2bb, Karlsruhe Document Collection.)

energy and determination warranted by its vital
importance. . . . The development and production
of the Me-262 has been attended by a number of
mysterious machinations - this sort of thing must
come to an end immediately! I refuse to let myself be lied to and deceived any longer!

Hereupon, the Fighter Staff established a new production schedule:
60 aircraft in July, 100 in August, 150 in September, 225 in October,
325 in November, and 500 in December.[77]

But even these figures were never to be achieved. By the end of
1944, the German aircraft industry had produced a grand total of 564
Me-262's. It was simply too late. Even Hitler's firm intercession
(as, for example, on 22 November)[78] came too late to have any influence.

For the purposes of this study, there is no point in our going into
the last desperate measures (such as the appointment of special representatives of the Fuehrer and of the Reichsmarschall for the jet fighter
program) which were initiated as the implacable waves of destruction
began to break over the Reich. During the first three months of 1945,
Germany achieved a total production of 740 jet fighters.

Germany had lost the race against time. Both Hitler and the leaders
of the Luftwaffe had taken far too long (from 1941 until 1943) to realize that a race against time was even involved. The time lost in the
delays prior to 1941 could no longer be recovered. And, in retrospect,
it seems clear that these delays in the field of aircraft engine development were of the greatest and most decisive importance. In the last
analysis, it was Milch's exaggerated (though, when one considers the
bitter experience behind him, perhaps warranted) skepticism, a certain
inexplicable aversion on the part of the Technical Office, and Hitler's
stubborn insistence on a superspeed bomber which combined to prevent the
timely production of the Me-262 fighter and--as a result--the establishment of air cover for the Reich. (Air cover for all of Europe was no
longer thinkable.) Timely production, in sufficient quantity, of the
Me-262 as a fighter aircraft not only would have prevented untold suffering on the part of the civilian population and enormous property destruction, but it might well have averted catastrophe in the scope which it
assumed in 1945. Saur, and his Fighter Staff, as well as Galland, whom
Saur called "father of the Me-262," did their best. Circumstances, however,--and here we must include Galland's unwillingness to accept the
limitations of reality and Saur's inability to overcome the desperation
of the overall situation--were simply such that they could no longer
succeed.

F O O T N O T E S

Chapter 1

1. See R. Suchenwirth, Goering als Oberbefehlshaber der deutschen Luftwaffe (Goering as Commander in Chief of the Luftwaffe), Karlsruhe
   Document Collection.

2. See also R. Suchenwirth, Erhard Milch, ein Versuch (Erhard Milch,
   An Essay), Karlsruhe Document Collection.

3. According to repeated assurances made to the author by Generalmajor
   a. D. Fritz Morzik (former Chief of the Air Transport Forces), the
   members of the air transport forces were well aware of Goering's
   attitude towards them.

4. See R. Suchenwirth, Hans Jeschonnek: Ein Versuch ueber Wesen, Wirken
   und Schicksal des vierten Generalstabchefs der deutschen Luftwaffe
   (Hans Jeschonnek, an Essay on the Character, Work, and Fate of the
   Fourth Chief of the Luftwaffe General Staff), Karlsruhe Document
   Collection.

5. See R. Suchenwirth, Ernst Udet, Generalluftzeugmeister der deutschen
   Luftwaffe (Ernst Udet, Chief of Procurement and Supply of the Luftwaffe), Karlsruhe Document Collection.

6. Generalleutnant a. D. Bruno Maass, Spitzengliederung der Luftwaffe
   waehrend der Aufbauzeit bis Kriegsbeginn (The Top-Level Command
   Organization of the Luftwaffe from its Founding until the Beginning
   of the War), Karlsruhe Document Collection; and the study The German
   Air Force General Staff, by Generalleutnant Andreas Nielsen. Both
   studies give expression to the attitudes held by members of the
   Luftwaffe General Staff.

7. During the course of a conversation with the author.

8. "A 100% National Socialist and unshakably loyal to Hitler . . .,"
   ". . . complete and uncritical obedience to Hitler" - General der
   Flieger Hans Georg von Seidel, the unfailingly objective former
   Quartermaster General of the Luftwaffe, used these phrases to
   describe Jeschonnek in a lecture delivered in Bonn during 1949.
   (Vortrag des ehemaligen Generalquartiermeisters der Luftwaffe,
   General d. Fl. a. D. von Seidel, F/I/b, Karlsruhe Document
   Collection.)

9. Based on a conversation between von Seidel and the author.

10. See J. W. Wheeler-Bennett, The Nemesis of Power, (London, 1953) whose basic tenor cannot be entirely brushed aside in spite of Waldemar Erfurth, Die Geschichte des deutschen Generalstabs von 1918-1945 (The History of the German General Staff from 1918 to 1945), (Goettingen, 1957).

11. Generalleutnant a. D. H. J. Rieckhoff, Trumpf oder Bluff: 12 Jahre deutscher Luftwaffe (Trump or Bluff - Twelve Years of the German Luftwaffe), (Geneva, 1945).

12. In this connection, see H. J. Rieckhoff's exaggerated and, quite probably, slanted comments, pp 22 ff in his Trumpf oder Bluff: 12 Jahre deutscher Luftwaffe.

13. Prophecy made to Goering by Hitler. Reported to the author by former State Secretary Paul Koerner on 19 September 1955. Koerner was a close and long time associate of Goering.

14. In the preparation of this section, the author has made frequent use of the study "Die Ausbildung in der deutschen Fliegertruppe" (Training in the German Luftwaffe), by Captain Gundelach, PhD, Karlsruhe Document Collection.

15. Jeschonnek expressed these opinions during a General Staff Trip /traditionally, an annual journey undertaken by the chief of the General Staff (prior to World War I the chief of the Great General Staff) with his staff officers to study tactical and strategic problems7 to the Rhineland in the spring of 1939. (Luftwaffen-kommando 3, Fuehrungsabteilung Nr. 2778/39 (Operations Branch No. 2778/39), F/I/2a, Karlsruhe Document Collection). For an opposing view, see Generalleutnant Hermann Plocher's report, Zur Organisa-tion der Luftwaffe (Concerning the Organization of the Luftwaffe), A/II/2a, Karlsruhe Document Collection.

16. In a speech before the commanders in chief of the Wehrmacht in the Reichs Chancellery in Berlin on 23 May 1939, F/I/1, Karlsruhe Docu-ment Collection.

17. B/III/1a, Karlsruhe Document Collection.

18. Unfortunately we have very little information about this very signi-ficant request and its fate. See Suchenwirth, Hans Jeschonnek, Ein Versuch ueber Wesen, Wirken und Schicksal des 4. Generalstabchefs der deutschen Luftwaffe (Hans Jeschonnek: an Essay on the Character, Work, and Fate of the Fourth Chief of the Luftwaffe General Staff), pp 39 ff.

19. During the air landing in Holland, 137 Ju-52's were lost. According to available figures, 145 Ju-52's were produced during the first four months of the war, 388 during 1940, and 502 during 1941. (Figures based on reports issued by Branch 6, Luftwaffe General Staff). These must be augmented by the number of aircraft released from repair.

20. Bericht des Generals d. Fl. a. D. Paul Deichmann ueber den Versuch, das Transportflugzeug Ju52 fuer die Ausbildung auf C-Fliegerschulen und Blindflugschulen auszuschaften (1956), (Report of General der Flieger a. D. Paul Deichmann on the attempt to have the air transport model (Ju52) eliminated as a training model in the C-schools and instrument flight schools), C/IV/2d, Karlsruhe Document Collection.

21. Letter from General von Seidel to General der Flieger a. D. Paul Deichmann under date of 9 November 1954, Karlsruhe Document Collection.

22. In September it was 122 bomber personnel and 161 fighter personnel; in October, 65 and 148; in November, 167 and 125; in December, 143 and 262; and in January 1943, 110 and 210. (Chef AW Nr. 155/43 g. Kdos. (Report, Chief of Training, #155/43, Classified), Karlsruhe Document Collection.)

23. See Die deutsche Reichsluftverteidigung 1933-45 (Germany's Home Air Defense, 1933-1945), by Generalmajor a. D. Walter Grabmann, Karlsruhe Document Collection. In Part II, Erfahrungen und Lehren der deutschen Luftverteidigung (The Experience Gained during German Home Air Defense Activity), p 1497, Generalmajor Grabmann speaks of a ratio of training hours of approximately 1:3 for the German and American fighter pilot.

24. Reported to the author during the course of a conversation with Milch on 28 September 1954.

25. See the report by Generalmajor a. D. Krauss (former commander of the 101st Bomber Group), Die Ausbildung im Bombenwurf und im Bomberzuenderwesen bei den Kampfverbaenden (ohne Ju-87-Verbaende) (The Training Carried out in Bomber Units in Bombardment and Bomb Detonation Techniques (exclusive of the Ju-87 Units)), Karlsruhe Document Collection. Hereinafter cited as "Krauss Report."

26. Ibid.

27. "Der Weg zur Luftschlacht um England in kriegsgerechtlicher Bedeutung" (The Battle of Britain and its Significance in Terms of International Military Law), by Eberhard Spetzler, Wehrwissenschaftlicher Rundschau (Military Science Survey), Frankfurt/Main, Volume 6, #8 (August 1956), p 442.

28. Krauss Report.

29. Ibid.

30. As Jeschonnek pointed out to Lt Col Deichmann on 1 October 1937, when the latter took over Branch I of the General Staff. (General der Flieger a. D. Paul Deichmann, in a post factum report, Warum verfugte Deutschland im 2. Weltkrieg ueber keinen brauchbaren viermotorigen Bomber? (Why Didn't Germany Have a Usuable Four-engine Bomber at Her Disposal During World War II?) 1953, C/IV/2cc, Karlsruhe Document Collection.)

31. See Die deutsche Luftwaffe im spanischen Buergerkreig - Legion Condor (The Role of the German Luftwaffe in the Spanish Civil War: the Condor Legion), by General der Flak a. D. Karl Drum, Karlsruhe Document Collection, pp 13, 51 and 53.

32. Generalmajor a. D. Fritz Morzik, Die Luftbrueckenunternehmungen der deutschen Luftwaffe: III Teil - Lehren und Erfahrungen (Luftwaffe Airlift Operations: Part III, Lessons Learned) p 11, Karlsruhe Document Collection. The underlining appears in the original.

33. Ibid., p 3.

34. Flugleistungstabelle der 6. Abt. des Generalstabes der Luftwaffe (Aircraft Technical Data, Branch 6, Luftwaffe General Staff) Karlsruhe Document Collection.

35. General a. D. Marquardt (Engineer Corps), in a paper entitled Die Stuka-Idee hat der deutschen Luftwaffe den Untergang gebracht (The Dive-Bomber Concept as the Ruin of the German Luftwaffe), Karlsruhe Document Collection. Hereinafter cited as Marquardt Study.

36. Ibid.

37. Ibid.

38. Stenografische Niederschrift der Besprechung beim Reichsmarschall ueber Flugzeug-Programme (stenographic record of a conference held by the Reichsmarschall on the aircraft program), C, (Karlsruhe Document Collection).

39. Jaegerstabsbesprechungen (fighter staff conference reports), C/I/2a, Karlsruhe Document Collection.

40. Ernst Heinkel, Stuermisches Leben (A Stormy Life), (Stuttgart, 1953), p 406.

41. Eberhard Schmidt, "Grundlagen und Wandlungen in der deutschen Flugzeugindustrie in den Jahren 1933-45" (The Basic Trends in the German Aircraft Industry during the Years 1933-1945 and the Changes Made during this Period), Flugwehr und Flugtechnik, (Zurich, 1949), Volume 2.

42. General der Flieger a. D. Wilhelm Wimmer, Kurze Angabe ueber die Geschichte des 4-motorigen Bombers (Brief Notes Concerning the History of the Four-Engine Bomber), 26 April 1956, Karlsruhe Document Collection.

43. General der Flieger a. D. Paul Deichmann, Warum verfuegte Deutschland im Zweiten Weltkrieg ueber keinen brauchbaren viermotorigen Bomber? (Why Did Germany have no Adequate Four-Engine Bomber at her Disposal during World War II?), Karlsruhe Document Collection. This very complete treatment of the subject, to which any detailed investigation of the problem must be deeply indebted, is based largely upon General Deichmann's own experience. For the purposes of the present study, a general acquaintance with the motivating factors in the development of the four-engine bomber is sufficient.

44. Ibid.

45. In a letter to General Deichmann dated 21 February 1954. See also the letter to Generalfeldmarschall Milch from Admiral a. D. Lahs, President of the Reichsverband der deutschen Luftfahrtindustrie (National Association of German Aircraft Manufacturers), file number 390/42, dated 2 November 1942, Karlsruhe Document Collection.

46. IMT, /International Military Tribunal7, Volume IX, p 72.

47. Generalingenieur a. D. Gerbert Huebner, Der tatsaechliche Ablauf der Aufgabenstellung (Planung) und Auswahl der Flugzeuge fuer die deutsche Luftwaffe (The True Course of Armament Planning and the Selection of Aircraft for the Luftwaffe), Karlsruhe Document Collection.

1. Generalingenieur a. D. Walter Hertel, Die Beschaffung in der deutschen Luftwaffe (Procurement in the German Luftwaffe), Karlsruhe
   Document Collection.

2. Ibid.

3. The total figure (all types of aircraft and including the conversion of older models and the repair of damaged machines) for the
   first four months of the war was 1367. The figures for 1940 and
   1941 were 16,665 and 13,379 respectively. In 1944 a total of
   44,738 aircraft (including new production, conversion, and repair)
   were taken over by the Generalquartiermeister (Quartermaster General). The figures for 1942 and 1943 were 17,987 and 28,420 respectively. (These figures are based on computations made by
   General Schulz, 8 July 1945, C/IV/2a, Karlsruhe Document Collection.)

4. We have only excerpts of this letter available, in the form of a
   copy made for the use of the von Rohden Project in England. The
   original, according to Lt Col Greffrath, who has been most intimately
   concerned with it, has been lost.

5. See footnote 4, above. Excerpts from the conference minutes, as
   well as of the Udet letter, are to be found in a four-page summary
   dealing with the "Development Stop of 1940/41," prepared by the von
   Rohden project group.

6. Taken from the summary text appended to the excerpts by von Rohden.
   The subquote might very well steam from Goering's thinking.

7. Bilanz des zweiten Weltkriegs: Erkenntnisse und Verpflichtungen
   fuer die Zukunft (The Balance Sheet of World War II; Experience
   Gained and its Application to the Future), (Oldenburg-Hamburg,
   1953), p 234.

8. Der Fuehrer und Oberste Befehlshaber der Wehrmacht, Nr. 340/41 g.
   Kdos. Chef OKW F.H.Qu. 11.9.1941 (The Fuehrer and Supreme Commander,
   Wehrmacht, No. 340/41, Classified; to the Chief, Wehrmacht High
   Command, Fuehrer's Headquarters, 11 September 1941); copy in Karls-
   ruhe Document Collection.

9. Der Reichsmarschall des Grossdeutschen Reiches und Oberbefehlshaber der Luftwaffe. Genst. Gen. Qu. 6 Abt., Nr. 7470/41 g. K. (I), (Reichs Marschall of the Pan-German Reich and Commander in Chief, Luftwaffe, No. 7470/41, Classified (I); to the Luftwaffe General Staff, Quartermaster General, Branch VI), Karlsruhe Document Collection.

10. Letter to the author dated 31 December 1957.

11. Based on information furnished the author on 3 September 1955 by Colonel Max Pendele, Retired, former adjutant of the Chief of Procurement and Supply.

12. The Halder Diary, under date of 31 July 1940.

13. OKW/WiRue Amt/Rue Ia Nr. 6710/40 g. vom 20.9.1940 (Wehrmacht High Command/Wehrmacht Armament Office/Armament Branch Ia, No. 6710/40, Classified, 20 September 1940), Karlsruhe Document Collection.

14. In a decree approved by Keitel on 23 December 1940, OKW, Chef Wi Rue Amt, Nr. 2959/40 g (Wehrmacht High Command, Chief, Wehrmacht Armament Office, No. 2959/40, Classified), Karlsruhe Document Collection.

15. This staff was founded at the suggestion of General von Richthofen. Its personnel was made up largely of officers and noncommissioned officers from the S-88 Staff of the Condor Legion. The new staff was assigned headquarters at Birkental, near Oppeln.

16. Taken from the diary of General von Richthofen, Karlsruhe Document Collection.

17. General der Flieger Paul Deichmann, Die Unterstuetzung des Heeres durch die deutsche Luftwaffe (Fliegertruppe) im 2. Weltkrieg (Close-Support Operations of the Luftwaffe during World War II), p 209, Karlsruhe Document Collection.

18. Copy in Karlsruhe Document Collection.

19. According to a notation in the Halder Diary under date of 22 July 1940.

20. Status as of 20 June 1941, immediately before the start of the Russian campaign, F/I/1d, Karlsruhe Document Collection.

21. Generalleutnant a. D. Hermann Plocher, Der Feldzug im Osten, 1941-1945, Viertes Buch, S. 483 (The Campaign in the East, Volume IV, p 483), Karlsruhe Document Collection.

FOOTNOTES

Chapter 3

1. In this connection, see the comments of "ear-witness" Generalleutnant Beppo Schmid, G/V/2d, Karlsruhe Document Collection.

2. OKW/WFA/L Nr. 33210/40 g.Kdos. (Wehrmacht High Command/Wehrmacht Operations Office/Luftwaffe, No. 33210/40, Classified), G/a, Karlsruhe Document Collection.

3. According to General der Flieger a. D. Josef Kammhuber, Hitler intended the air war against England as a gambit to force her to negotiate for peace, not as a "decisive test of strength." In Kammhuber's opinion, Goering was aware even then of the coming conflict with Russia and its implications for the Luftwaffe. (Das Problem der Erringung der Luftherrschaft durch Gegenmassnahmen der deutschen Luftwaffe (The Problem of Attaining Air Supremacy through Countermeasures by the German Air Force), Part II, page 11 ff, underlining taken from the original), Karlsruhe Document Collection.

4. Ob.d.L. Fuehrungsstab Ic Nr. 5835/40 g.Kdos. (Commander in Chief, Luftwaffe/Operations Staff, No. 5835/40, Classified), G/V/3g, Karlsruhe Document Collection.

5. Reports maintained by the Office of the Quartermaster General, C/IV/2a, Karlsruhe Document Collection.

6. Dr. Theo Weber, "Die Luftschlacht um England in historischer Sicht" (The Battle of Britain in an Historical Perspective), Flugwehr und Technik, (first half of 1954) page 177. Dr. Weber, in turn, bases his figures on Winston Churchill, Der Zweite Weltkrieg (The Second World War - German edition), (Bern, 1947-53) Volume II, Book II, p 31.

7. Ibid., p 93.

8. Ibid.

9. General der Flieger a. D. Josef Kammhuber, Das Problem der Erringung der Luftherrschaft durch Gegenmassnachmen der deutschen Luftwaffe (The Problem of Obtaining Air Supremacy through Countermeasures by the Luftwaffe), Part II, p 11 ff.

10. The Halder Diary, under date of 31 July 1940; Karlsruhe Document Collection.

11. This, as well as that which follows, is taken from Goering's testimony at Nuremberg; IMT, Volume IX, pp 382-388.

12. Information given to the author during the course of a conversation with State Secretary Koerner on 19 September 1955. The subsequent quotes from Goering are also based on information furnished by Koerner.

13. Ibid.

14. Plocher, Campaign in the East, Volume I, p 178 ff.

15. Ibid., p 187.

16. "Dienstvorschrift der deutschen Luftwaffe ueber die Luftkriegfuehrung," usually abbreviated as L. Dv. 16. Copy in F/I/2a, Karlsruhe Document Collection.

17. Der Reichsminister und Oberbefehlshaber der Luftfahrt, Chef des Ministeramtes, Min. A. Nr. 597/38 g.Kdos. Berlin 20.9.1938 (Reichs Minister and Commander in Chief, Aviation, Chief of the Ministry Office, Air Ministry, No. 597/38, Classified, Berlin, 20 September 1938), C/IV/2b, Karlsruhe Document Collection.

18. Plocher, Campaign in the East, Book II, Der Vernichtungsschlag gegen die sowjetische Fliegertruppe (The Annihilating Blow against the Russian Air Forces), pp 2-22.

19. Eike Middeldorf, Taktik im Russlandfeldzug. Erfahrungen und Folgerungen (The Tactics of the Russian Campaign; Experience Gained and Conclusions Drawn), Mittler & Sohn, (Berlin and Frankfurt, 1956).

20. Plocher, Campaign in the East, Book III, p 71.

21. Ibid., p 79.

22. For an example see 12.6.1943. Der Chef der Luftflotte 6. Br.B.Nr. 241/43 g.Kdos./Chefsache (12 June 1943, Commanding Officer, Sixth Air Fleet, Branch B, No. 241/43, Classified), G/VI/4d, Karlsruhe Document Collection.

23. No. 477621/452, G/VI/5b, Karlsruhe Document Collection.

24. Luftwaffenfuehrungsstab Ia op Nr. 8865/43 g.Kdos. Chefsache. Anlage: Kurze Studie: Kampf gegen die russische Ruestungsindustrie (Luftwaffe

Operations Staff/Operations Officer, No. 8865/43, Classified.
Appendix: Brief Study: The Campaign Against the Russian Armaments
Industry), Karlsruhe Document Collection.

25. Angriffe des IV. Fliegerkorps vom 27.3.1944-22.7.1944 auf russiche
Bahnhoefe, aus Geschwadergeschichte des K.G.4. (The Attacks Carried
out by the IV Air Corps on Russian Railway Stations during the
Period 27 March through 22 July 1944, from the History of the 4th
Bomber Wing), H/V/1, Karlsruhe Document Collection.

26. Ibid.

27. Major R. T. Gilchrist, Malta Strikes Back; The Story of the 231st
Infantry Brigade, (Aldershot, no year), pp 1, 2.

28. These figures are based on Rudolf Boehmler, "Das Unternehmen Malta
fand nicht statt" (Operation MALTA Did Not Take Place), in Der
deutsche Fallschirmjaeger (The German Paratrooper), No. 8, 1956,
copy in G/VII/9, Karlsruhe Document Collection. Hereinafter cited
as Boehmler Report. Admiral Ruge gives a total of 776,000 tons as
having been sunk by submarines in the Mediterranean by September
1943, in addition to 774,000 tons destroyed by enemy aircraft. His
data indicate that Malta-based operations accounted for two-thirds
of the total damage. Ruge, Der Seekrieg 1939-1945 (The Naval War,
1939-1945), (Stuttgart, 1954), p 192.

29. "Der beabsichtigte Angriff auf Malta" (The Projected Attack on Malta),
in Der deutsche Fallschirmjaeger (The German Paratrooper), No. 10,
1956; copy in G/VII/9, Karlsruhe Document Collection.

30. Kesselring, Soldat bis zum letzten Tag (Soldier to the End),(Bonn,
1953), p 148.

31. Boehmler Report.

32. General der Flieger a. D. Paul Deichmann, "Luftlandeaktion Malta"
(Air Landing Operations on Malta), G/VII/9, Karlsruhe Document
Collection.

33. Ibid.

34. Kesselring, Soldat bis zum letzten Tag, p 166.

35. Enno von Rintelen, Mussolini als Bundesgenosse (Mussolini as an
Ally), (Tuebingen, 1951), p 166 ff.

36. _Ibid._

37. _The Ciano Diaries, 1939-1943_, Edited by Hugh Gibson, (New York, 1946), pp 477 and 492.

38. Kesselring, p 167.

39. Rintelen, p 170 ff.

40. Published in _Der deutsche Fallschirmjaeger_ (The German Paratrooper), No. 11 (October), 1956, Copy in G/VII/9, Karlsruhe Document Collection.

41. _Die deutsche Luftwaffe im Mittelmeer (Auszuege aus Schriften des Jahres 1945 (nach der Kapitulation) von General Koller und Oberst Bernd v. Brauchitsch)_ /The Luftwaffe in the Mediterranean (Extracts from a post-war report, (1945) by General Koller and Colonel Bernd v. Brauchitsch/, G/VII/1, Karlsruhe Document Collection.

42. Kesselring, p 173.

43. Deichmann, _Malta_, G/VII/9, Karlsruhe Document Collection.

44. _Ibid._

45. See Hitler's reservations and doubts (expressed on 16 September, 25 October, and 2 November 1942), as collected by Helmut Greiner, _Die oberste Wehrmachtsfuehrung 1939-1943_ (The Armed Forces Top-Level Command, 1939-1943), (Wiesbaden, 1951), p 410 ff.

46. See the von Richthofen diary, under date of 27 August 1942, G/VI/4d, Karlsruhe Document Collection.

47. Plocher, _Campaign in the East_, Book IV, p 205.

48. In a teletype message dispatched at 1815 on 23 November 1942. Message reproduced in Hans Doerr /Generalmajor a. D./ _Der Feldzug nach Stalingrad_, E.S. Mittler & Sohn Gmbh, (Darmstadt, 1955), p 72, no source given.

49. Detlev Herhudt von Rohden, _Die Luftwaffe ringt um Stalingrad_ (The Luftwaffe's Struggle for Stalingrad), (Wiesbaden, 1950), p 36.

50. _Ibid._, p 33.

51. This figure is based on von Rohden, p 76. General Plocher estimates an average of 102 tons daily for the period 25 November 1942 through 11 January 1943. (Plocher, Book IV, p 4)

52. Plocher, Book IV, p 290.

53. These figures, including aircraft totally destroyed, missing, or damaged beyond the point of salvage, are based on Plocher, p 482, who in turn credits them to an entry in the Milch diary dated 2 February 1943, as cited by von Rohden, p 140. These losses include those sustained by the 4th Bomber Wing (see the report prepared by General der Flieger a. D. Paul Deichmann, G/VI/4d, Karlsruhe Document Collection).

54. Based on Hitler's comments to Feldmarschall von Manstein on 5 February 1943, von Manstein, Verlorene Siege (Lost Victories), (Bonn, 1955), p 395.

55. Karl Koller, Der letzte Monat (The Last Month), diary of the last General Staff Chief of the Luftwaffe for the period 14 April through 27 May 1945, (Mannheim, 1949), p 40.

56. See Generalmajor a. D. Walter Grabmann, Die deutsche Luftverteidigung 1933-1945 (German Home Air Defense Operations from 1933 to 1945), Karlsruhe Document Collection--a well-founded and extremely informative treatise (1675 pages). Hereinafter cited as Grabmann Study.

57. Grabmann Study, p 1509.

58. Ibid., p 1093.

59. Ibid., p 1184.

60. Ltr., Willy Messerschmitt to Walter Grabmann, 24 Aug 55, copy in Karlsruhe Document Collection, C/IV/2bb.

61. Brief, General der Jagdflieger am Oberbefehlshaber der Luftwaffe, 25 Mai 1943 (Ltr General of the Fighter Forces to Commander in Chief, Luftwaffe, 25 May 1943) signed Galland. Copy in C/IV/2bb, Karlsruhe Document Collection.

62. Ibid. Underlining by author of this study.

63. Decision of 2 June 1943 mentioned in Generalluftzeugmeisterbesprechung (Chief of Procurement and Supply Conference) of 10 June 1943. Quotation is from Erhard Milch, Ibid., C/IV/2bb, Karlsruhe Document Collection.

64. GL. - Sitzungsbericht (Chief of Procurement and Supply Proceedings) 17 Aug 1943, C/IV/2bb, Karlsruhe Document Collection.

65. Die deutschen Jagdflugzeuge 1939-1945 (The German Fighter Aircraft from 1939 to 1945), by Generalleutnant a. D. Adolph Galland, C/IV/2bb, Karlsruhe Document Collection.

66. Die geplante Verwendung der Me 262 als Schnellbomber (The Planned Employment of the Me 262 as a High-Speed Bomber), extract from a conference on 2 Nov 1943 on the occasion of Goering's visit with Messerschmitt. This is probably a stenographic record, C/IV/2bb, Karlsruhe Document Collection.

67. Die geplante Verwendung der Me 262 als Schnellbomber, C/IV/2bb, Karlsruhe Document Collection.

68. Quoted in Die Entwicklung des Strahl - und Raketenflugzeuges, (The Development of Jet and Rocket Aircraft), (von Rohden Project), C/IV/2bb, Karlsruhe Document Collection.

69. Ibid.

70. Adj. d. Wehrmacht beim Fuehrer, Ia v. Below, Oberstlt., Br. B. Nr. 650-43 g.Kdos, 5.12.1943, (Wehrmacht Aide to the Fuehrer, Operations Section, Lt. Col. von Below, Branch B, No. 650-43, Classified, dated 5 December 1943), C/IV/2bb, Karlsruhe Document Collection.

71. Baumbach, p 93 ff.

72. Ibid., p 94.

73. Besprechung RM Goering am 29.5.44./Obersalzberg (Conference, Reichsmarschall Goering, 29 May 44/Obersalzberg), Karlsruhe Document Collection, C/IV/2bb, (F/2d).

74. The Kreipe Diary, entry of 30 August 1944, H/I/3, Karlsruhe Document Collection.

75. Punkte aus Fuehrerbesprechungen November 1944, Reichsminister Speer (Notes from a Fuehrer Conference, Nov 1944, Reichsminister Speer), C/IV/2bb, Karlsruhe Document Collection.

76. Jaegerstabbesprechung, 22.6.1944 (Fighter Staff Conference, 22 June 1944), C/IV/2bb, Karlsruhe Document Collection.

77. Der Reichsminister fuer Ruestung und Kriegsproduktion, Jaegerstab,
    Bericht ueber die Me 262, 23.6.1944, g.Kdos. (Reichsminister for
    Armament and War Production, Fighter Staff, Report on the Me 262,
    23 June 1944, Classified), C/IV/2bb, Karlsruhe Document Collection.

78. Kurzberichten des Ruestungsstabes, 22.11.44 (Brief Reports of the
    Armaments Staff, 22 Nov 44), C/IV/2bb, Karlsruhe Document Collection.

Appendix 1

LIST OF EQUIVALENT LUFTWAFFE
AND USAF GENERAL OFFICER RANKS

Reichsmarschall des Grossdeutschen   No equivalent
Reiches (Goering's rank: Reichs
Marshall of the Pan-German Reich)

Generalfeldmarschall   General of the Air Force (Army)

Generaloberst   General

General der Flieger   Lieutenant General
(der Flak, etc.)

Generalleutnant   Major General

Generalmajor   Brigadier General

    The initials a.D. /ausser Dienst/ given between an officer's rank
and his name indicate "retired" status.

Appendix 2

LIST OF GAF MONOGRAPH PROJECT STUDIES

Study No.	Title
150	The German Air Force in the Spanish War
151	The German Air Force in Poland
152	The German Air Force in France and the Low Countries (including Airlanding Operations in Belgium and the Netherlands)
153-155	The German Air Force versus Russia on the Eastern Front
156	The Battle of Britain
157	Operation Sea Lion
158-160	The German Air Force versus the Allies in the West
161	The German Air Force versus the Allies in the Mediterranean
162	The Battle of Crete
163 & 165	German Air Force Close Support and Air Interdiction Operations
164	German Air Force Air Defense Operations
166	German Air Force Counter Air Operations
167	German Air Force Airlift Operations
168	German Air Force Air-Sea Rescue Operations
169	Training in the German Air Force
170	Procurement in the German Air Force
171	Intelligence in the German Air Force
172	German Air Force Medicine

Study No.	Title
173	The German Air Force General Staff
174	Command and Leadership in the German Air Force (Goering, Milch, Jeschonnek, Udet, Wever)
175	The Russian Air Force in the Eyes of German Commanders
176	Russian Patterns of Reaction to the German Air Force
177	Russian Use of Airlift to Supply Partisan Forces
178	Problems of Fighting a Three-Front Air War
179	Problems of Waging a Day and Night Defensive Air War
180	The Problem of the Long-Range Night Intruder Bomber
181	The Problem of Air Superiority in the Battle with Allied Strategic Air Forces
182	Fighter-Bomber Operations in Situations of Air Inferiority
183	Analysis of Specialized Anglo-American Techniques
184	Effects of Allied Air Attacks on German Divisional and Army Organizations on the Battle Fronts
185	Effects of Allied Air Attacks on German Air Force Bases and Installations
186	The German Air Force System of Target Analysis
187	The German Air Force System of Weapons Selection
188	German Civil Air Defense
189	Historical Turning Points in the German Air Force War Effort
190	The Organization of the German Air Force High Command and Higher Echelon Headquarters within the German Air Force